Becoming
the
Master's Key

L. Emerson Ferrell

E&A
International

E & A INTERNATIONAL
Becoming the Master's Key
1st Edition
3rd Printing

Cover design:
Ruben Mariaca Asport, areyou_ben@hotmail.com

Interior design:
*osprey*design, www.ospreydesign.com

All scripture quotations unless otherwise indicated are taken from the King James Version

Printing:
United Graphics, Inc.

Category:
Prophetic Teaching

Publisher:
E & A INTERNATIONAL
P.O. Box 3418
Ponte Vedra Florida 32004
www.voiceofthelight.com

ISBN: ISBN 1-933163-06-2

Dedication

I would like to dedicate this book first and foremost to the precious Holy Spirit. He has been more faithful to me than I merit or deserve. My heart is so full of gratitude and thanksgiving that words can not express.

I can not begin to thank my dear wife Ana whose selfless work has made this book a reality. Thank you sweetheart. "I pray God will reward you abundantly for your encouragement and perseverance."

Special thanks to my son Jordan whose faith in his dad also did not go unnoticed.

Contents

Prologue

I believe that this book, *Becoming The Masters Key*, written by Emerson Ferrell, a teacher and intercessor, helps us to understand which keys are needed to achieve a victorious Christian life.

The first three keys, giving, fasting, and prayer are essential for the body of Christ. Unfortunately, although these are important, few Christians practice them. I truly believe that when you finish reading this book you will clearly understand the meaning of these keys, which will help you achieve success in your spiritual walk.

I am sure that Emerson Ferrell was inspired by the Lord to teach us, not only the first three keys of the Kingdom, but also how to fight against the spirit of Mammon. I know that after you finish reading this book, you will rise to the next level in your spiritual giving, fasting and prayer. You will also learn how to overcome the spirit of Mammon.

The person who reads this book will be transformed and changed by it. I am a witness to the fact that the author of this book practices what he teaches, daily, and with diligence. That is why this book is so informative, and above all, filled with God's revelation in each of its chapters.

This is an great book and I already want the first copy for myself!

—*Guillermo Maldonado, Pastor and Apostle*
El Rey Jesus International Ministry

Introduction

Those of us who believe the Church is ready to move into a new era of reformation may find this book to offer solid footing for such a venture. For those who believe the Church is, according to statistics growing quite nicely and should continue its direction and message might not find this book to appealing.

In Matthew 6:24 and Luke 16:13 Jesus said, "You cannot serve God and Mammon." We will endeavor to understand what that statement means as it relates to our Church and daily lives. We will expose our spirits to the truth of the Word of God and how to identify whom we serve. The truth is what makes us free according to the Scriptures and the designs of the Holy Spirit will be our guide.

I believe the Lord is speaking to all of us who "have ears to hear," a message of reformation and transformation. One of the messages the Church is receiving is to "come out of Babylon." I have heard many ministers and lay people speaking this word.

Babylon has many meanings. Some say it is the Church structure of religion, others say it is corruption in the Churches, etc. Both of these are true and relevant. However, this book will speak about the spirit which is behind all the definitions of Babylon. That spirit is mammon and it is so malevolent that our very lives are being sacrificed to this spirit without us even knowing about it. I believe this is what is spoken of in Revelation 18:2:

> He gave a mighty shout, "Babylon the Great is fallen, is fallen; she has become a den of demons, a haunt of devils and every kind of evil spirit. For all the nations have drunk the fatal wine of her intense immorality. The rulers of earth have enjoyed themselves with her, and businessmen throughout the world have grown rich from all her luxurious living.

As I said earlier we will endeavor to uncover keys located in Matthew chapter 6 that will help us destroy this spirit in our lives. I believe all of us, with no exception, have drunk of the fatal wine, and become addicted to this insidious spirit. The goal of this spirit is to kill, steal and destroy our destiny in God.

Through the mercy and grace of the precious Holy Spirit, I have been privileged to see the awesome design of God for victory over this enemy. During extensive fasting, the Holy Spirit opened my eyes to see some truths that can radically transform our lives. I am not speaking about a temporary spiritual band aid. I am talking about walking into realms of understanding that you may not have been privileged to see. I am not being spiritually arrogant when I tell you; through times of great ecstasy with the Lord I was shown "the beginning from the end of this matter."

The important thing for all of us to know is, what you are about to read comes with a warning label. That label reads, "You have now been given the blue print to become armed and dangerous against this devil. What you do with this revelation will determine how you finish your course. It is that serious."

This book will detail the importance of giving, praying and fasting. You will be given insight on how to achieve victory over those particular areas in your life. The keys you receive can actually be used to unlock the deepest parts of your souls. "You desire truth in the inward being; therefore teach me wisdom in my secret heart" (Psalm 51:6).

These places within our hearts, minds and souls are what have made us slaves to mammon and not stewards in Gods kingdom.

The places Job learned about from God is what transformed his very soul (Job 4:12 Living Bible).

This truth was given me in secret, as though whispered in my ear. It came in a nighttime vision as others slept. Suddenly, fear gripped me; I trembled and shook with terror, as a spirit passed before my face—my hair stood up on end. I felt the spirit's presence, but couldn't see it standing there. Then out of the dreadful silence came this voice:

"Is mere man more just than God? More pure than his Creator?"

"If God cannot trust his own messengers (for even angels make mistakes), how much less men made of dust, who are crushed to death as easily as moths!" They are alive in the morning, but by evening they are dead, gone forever with hardly a thought from anyone. Their candle of life is snuffed out. They die and no one cares.

Has anyone preached the message of "Fearing God is the Beginning of Wisdom," in the Churches of late? It seems to me I hear many messages about how God loves me, wants me to prosper and have the good life while here on earth. But I have not heard much about "the fear of God" being the beginning of everything in my Christian life.

We will speak about the wisdom of God and how it is revealed to those who have such a reverent fear of God that serving any other God but the God of Abraham, Isaac and Jacob is not an option.

The Church is not where Jesus left it 2000 years ago. It has been reshaped and reformed to many cultural and social issues. None of which have shaped it after His Image. His Image is something that was lost in the Garden of Eden but reformed in the Garden of Gethsemane. We are going to discover how to return to that image through our discussion.

If when you are finished reading this book you can honestly repent from serving mammon and return to your first love with all your heart, my mission has been accomplished. This will only be the beginning of a life time of battles with this spirit. But you have been equipped by the Holy Spirit; the word of God and the design God has placed inside of you to be victorious.

1
Giving:
The First Key

Let us begin our journey by under-standing our purpose. There is nothing more miserable than to drive off in some direction without first knowing where that direction leads or if the road we are currently on will take us to a desired destination.

One thing was certain about our Lord; He knew where He was going and the best way to get there and the thing that very few of us understand the driving force that made Him give His life as the ultimate reconciliation for us, to access the Father.

The major purpose of our journey is to unlock the mystery of that power and to unfold these truths through the "keys" hidden in the scriptures. We will begin by uncovering Matthew chapter six.

Most people are aware that chapters and verses, in the Bible are arranged by the translators. This can sometimes create a separation of continuity and thought structures.

Yet, even the Holy Spirit has been known to rearrange things in the minds and hearts of people, including the translators to suit His needs.

I believe in the way this chapter is designed, the location of the texts and the position of the "keys" are very significant. I hope you will see the wisdom behind the order of this chapter and the choice of words used by Jesus.

So, the purpose is to understand this chapter in a simple and yet profound way. This will allow the Holy Spirit to release a new understanding in the Body of Christ. The reason for this is to sustain a powerful new reformation that is being released.

I have found at least three major keys that unlock doors. These doors have been closed to all of us from time to time in our Christian lives. They are simple doors of giving, praying and fasting.

The profoundness is released individually, to each one of us who unlock these doors. Once those doors have been opened, a new vision is released by the Holy Spirit, to reveal even deeper truths. These truths begin to give us insight into the driving force of our Lord while on this planet.

Let's begin with the first key.

Giving: The First Key

By opening to the first verse of Chapter Six of Matthew, we find Jesus telling His disciples and all those listening, including the Pharisees:

Take heed that ye do not your alms before men, to be seen of them: otherwise ye have no reward of your Father which is in heaven. Therefore when thou doest thine alms, do not sound a trumpet before thee, as the hypocrites do in the synagogues and in the streets, that they may have glory of men. Verily I say unto you, They have their reward. But when thou doest alms, let not thy left hand know what thy right hand doeth: That thine alms may be in secret: and thy Father which seeth in secret himself shall reward thee openly.

Since Jesus begins by talking about giving, in the form of alms, we need to define some terms.

Let us begin by understanding what "alms" means. One source, Nelson's illustrated Bible dictionary defines it this way: "money given out of mercy for the poor." This source goes on to say, "by Jesus' time, the word "righteousness" was tied closely to the word "alms.""

So we might paraphrase the first verse by saying that when we give, in order to be counted righteous, our motive should be to please God and not man. Jesus implies that giving is expected but the motive behind the gift is most important.

I believe Jesus is teaching this to reveal a much deeper truth. Jesus is saying that the very beginning stage of our development, as a disciple is determined by how and why we give.

Jesus said later in the same book of Matthew, in 26:11 that the poor will always be around. So, giving to the poor is not the main issue, it is the heart He is after. The poor are the visible means by which our hearts are being tried; money becomes a way to measure our obedience.

Jesus will ask every one of us if we understand the price that has been paid for our salvation.

He asks this through many ways, but the most basic is through our tithes and offerings. The issue of giving is elementary to each of us who know the price Jesus paid. If we have not gone to depths of understanding the cross and the price associated with our Savior, then giving will always be a problem.

Giving is so much more than leaving your money in an envelope or offering plate. True giving comes from an attitude that understands the depth of what our Lord and Savior has done. True giving is determined not only by the amount we bring before the Lord but by the amount we keep for ourselves.

Our demonstration of gratitude is meant to be a continual offering before God in every part of our life. For example, parents don't give to their children because of rules established by books and experts. Parents give because they are flesh and blood of their offspring and the needs of their children are more important than their own. This type of relationship is what makes the family a family and creates harmony and security among its members.

We find this type of relationship or covenant all through scripture. So when God made covenant with man He knew man could never keep this level of commitment so what did He do?

> For when God made a promise to Abraham, because He could swear by no one greater, He swore by Himself, saying, "Surely blessing I will bless you, and multiplying I will multiply you." And so, after he had patiently endured, he obtained the promise. For men indeed swear by the greater, and an oath for confirmation is for them an end of all disputes. Thus God, determining to show more abundantly to the heirs of promise the immutability of His counsel, confirmed it by an oath, that by two immutable things, in which it is impossible for God to lie.
>
> —*Hebrews 6:13-18*

This is the type of love that produces passion in one's heart to give all. This type of giving comes from the understanding that nothing I have belongs to me.

Absolutely all of us, every breathe we take, every beat of our heart, is through the profound mercy of God. When that realization consumes us, the struggle over why and how much to give becomes no struggle. We are in submission to the Holy Spirit. If the truth that God has pledged Himself to our success becomes a reality, the pursuit of our selfish agenda becomes abnormal and living totally for Him becomes the normal life for us.

Think with me for a minute. The creator of the entire universe has made covenant with you through Jesus. Part of that covenant, just a small part, is His pledge to take care of you as you would take care of your own children. Let me ask those of you who are parents, "Would you provide every good and perfect gift within your means to your offspring?" The answer is obvious, "of course."

Is our heavenly Father capable to provide more than we possibly could? Absolutely, yet in the average Christian life "giving" seems to be a major area of not trusting God. This is why it is the first subject Jesus speaks about in this chapter.

For some "twisted" reason, we believe we can make better decisions with our finances than He can. If we will observe this hypocrisy in our lives and purpose to repent from this belief structure the Holy Spirit is then capable of revealing even deeper truths about the nature of our trust and belief systems.

Perhaps this is why there has been so much teaching on faith, particularly in the area of our finances. I totally applaud those who have been at the forefront of that message and have done their best to train us in the scriptures concerning faith. This has prepared us to move beyond just sowing and reaping.

In my life I have observed my faith in the beginning, which was measured in dollars, to being measured in obedience. The amount becomes secondary to the willingness to becoming someone the Father can trust.

No greater example is given in the Old Testament than Abraham and Isaac:

Now it came to pass after these things that God tested Abraham, and said to him, "Abraham!" And he said, "Here I am." Then He said, "Take now your son, your only son Isaac, whom you love, and go to the land of Moriah, and offer him there as a burnt offering on one of the mountains of which I shall tell you."

—Genesis 22:1-2

This offering had nothing to do with money and everything to do with value. In our life we sometimes do not even get to the place of giving the most precious "thing" we posses as Abraham did.

For example, when was the last time your giving could ultimately have resulted in loss of your life? Or what have you given that resulted in your total trust in God for your very existence?

This type of obedience requires such a deep understanding of our relationship to our Father that life as we know it on this planet radically changes. Tomorrow has no meaning other than "how can I please the One who gave me this day and the very breath I am breathing?"

This key of "giving" is the first and most important because without it no other key is available to us. This is why if we just think of it in terms of money we have totally misunderstood our Lord; our Heavenly Father demonstrated why to give and what amount to give in John 3:16.

For God so loved the world that He gave His only begotten Son, that whoever believes in Him should not perish but have everlasting life. For God did not send His Son into the world to condemn the world, but that the world through Him might be saved.

— *John 3:16-17*

The true standard of giving is set by the One, whom through our conversion, requires our life for His. If we do not understand the price paid by our Father, our ability to give is dramatically diminished. This is why a constant reminder of the cross is so critical for our repentance of anything associated with selfishness. I believe, giving is the first and most powerful key to understand.

Our opening verse speaks about giving in secret, which causes God to reward the giver in open.

In 1 Corinthians 2:7 Paul said what God did was a mystery to the powers in control of this planet. Paul was of course speaking of the crucifixion of Jesus that was done in secret dethroning the "powers and principalities of this world."

And just like Jesus revealed in Matthew 6:4, God is now rewarding Himself openly with a future bride for His Son.

Can you see the wisdom and beauty of this design? His love for mankind was so deep and the pain of separation so intense that He gave the best gift He had with the purest of motives, in secret. Now what has been done in secrete is bearing fruit for the entire world to see. The true bride is being displayed for the entire world to see. This fruit, called the "Body of Christ" will begin to build the foot stool for Jesus to rest His feet.

The LORD says to you, my lord: "Take your throne at my right-hand, while I make your enemies your footstool."

—*Psalm 110:1*

Beloved we are living in the most outstanding period of history. Jesus is preparing a perfect "Body" that will move through this earth like a hot knife through butter. The revelation that is being poured out right now will equip all who are willing to destroy the works of the enemy. This army will move into a level of faith that we all have read about in the Scriptures. The faith of the giants recorded in Hebrews will become realized by a generation that understands the keys of the kingdom being released at this time in history.

Let's look at the supernatural force behind faith and how it is released:

But without faith it is impossible to please Him, for he who comes to God must believe that He is, and that He is a rewarder of those who diligently seek Him.

—*Hebrews 11:6*

We will continue to see how God is a rewarder, but not everyone today is coming with the purest of motives.

Our Heavenly Father wants every human being to experience Him as more than willing and able to take care of our every need. His method of showing us this is demonstrated by our willingness to trust Him (faith) in the secret place (unseen).

We will keep returning to the motives of our heart. If we truly have experienced the depth, width, height and length (or dimensions) of the love of Christ, our motives will move from the seen realm to the unseen realm. The unseen realm requires a currency called faith to access the Father. One translation of Hebrews 11 says, "Faith means being sure of the things we hope for and knowing that something is real even if we do not see it."

Any growth we make in the unseen realm is always by faith. **We must give what we can see as a deposit in the realm we cannot see.** Then the Father, knowing how we train children, gives us a reward to reinforce our efforts of faith. Then He will train us to totally trust Him with everything we hold valuable, as He did Abraham.

This is why Jesus began the chapter with the most elementary key called "giving." If we can not understand this level or are not willing to give back to Him everything He has entrusted to us, it will be impossible to receive the next "key."

Remember, each key is critical if we are to advance beyond our ineffective Christian lives to enter the heavenly places God has provided for us through Jesus. These "places" require "keys" to unlock doors that have been shut as a result of our disobedient ancestors, beginning with Adam. Jesus came that we might have abundant life which is far beyond "big houses and cars." Look what

Jesus said in John 10:10. A thief comes to steal and kill and destroy, but I came to give life—life in all its fullness.

This is the life of watching the Father, as Jesus did, doing as He does, and obeying as He did. Jesus knew that on earth there would be many different circumstances and influences continually bidding for His attention, but He knew His purpose, and that kept Him focused. But He also knew that His Father was the sole authority in His life, and if He watched His Father, there would be no surprises from the thief.

Jesus is our role model, and everything He said and did were examples or demonstrations of how to live for the Father. This would be impossible without the Holy Spirit, but Jesus knew that and made arrangements for the precious Holy Spirit to take us into even greater dimensions than He Himself.

As a parent, I want my son to go farther and reach higher than me and that is what Jesus said, "Greater works shall you do." What a wonderful Savior is ours.

There are many different levels of giving, but we will look at only three.

1. Giving To Get

Most Christians are taught that God is a giver and He will always give you more than you give Him. The "prosperity" message has built large Churches and filled big auditoriums with Christians looking for a better life and thrilled with the idea of lots of money. All the Scriptures quoted by the so-called "prosperity" crowd are legitimate and indeed speak of the desire of the Father to take care of His children, royally.

> A good man leaveth an inheritance to his children's children: and the wealth of the sinner is laid up for the just.
>
> —*Proverbs 13:22*

Unfortunately, this scripture has made many believers passionate for their "inheritance" from the wicked. But there has been very little transfer and even less impact made in the world of the unbeliever.

It is not my intention to be critical of those who have preached these messages for all these years. Nor am I attempting to belittle those who have "confessed" their promises.

What I am saying is that there is a bigger reality that truly works for those of us who want to be wealthy stewards of the Kingdom of God. But the entrance to this higher level must be through the gate of self denial and the cross. Then we qualify to handle a transfer of wealth from the heathen to the "just." This is what is being described in the Scripture as one who is righteous and lives by faith.

> For in it the righteousness of God is revealed from faith to faith; as it is written, The just shall live by faith.

The faith message is real, that God wants to bless His children is true. The problem has always been the "heart." God loves all of us but, He only can trust those who trust Him. Let's look at a very interesting scripture beginning in Luke 16:11.

> Therefore if you have not been faithful in the unrighteous Mammon, who will commit to your trust the true riches? And if you have not been faithful in what is another man's, who will give you what is your own? No servant can serve two masters; for either he will hate the one and love the other, or else he will be loyal to the one and despise the other. You cannot serve God and Mammon.
>
> —*Luke 16:11-13*

Notice that Jesus makes it clear in the text that if we can not be trusted with unrighteous Mammon, how can we receive the true riches? The prosperity message has been derelict in teaching that the money of this world is strictly a test or way of measuring a true believer's heart.

People who run after the wealth of this world unfortunately have little understanding of how abominable that is to our Lord.

Some teachers of Scriptures and followers believe that if you do not have lots of money, you have not achieved the level of God that people with money have. Nothing could be farther from the truth. God is interested in the heart; always has and always will be. The heart is the true compass of our motives.

The rest of that Scripture tells us that you can not serve two masters. Notice, Satan is not mentioned as a master. So this other master must be a spirit to be compared with God and it must desire worship in some way.

In her book "Seated in Heavenly Places," Ana Mendez Ferrell talks about this subject in some detail:

> Mammon has a kingdom and a terribly strong structure with which he dominates the kingdoms of the earth and a vast majority of Christians. This spirit governs in a subtle way and is very difficult to detect by the people of God. Unfortunately, being ignorant of his devices is one of the principle causes that impede us from possessing what is ours.

The book goes on to describe that the purpose of this spirit called Mammon is to destroy our confidence in God and subtly cause us to submit to it. Mammon has a voice. If we could identify it, the conversation might sound like the following:

> I am your master; I control your finances, your emotions. I am the one who tells you what you can do and what you can't do. I determine where you can travel, and if you can travel. I determine where you can buy your clothes, what restaurants you can go to and which ones you can't. I am the one who says how you can treat the servants of God and what you can do and not do for them. I am the one who decides how much you can give for an offering and

how much you can tithe, or even if you should tithe at all. I decide what school your children go to and to which hospital you can take your family. Remember, I am the one who makes your budget, and I determine what you can do and what you can't, because I am your master. When you must make a decision concerning money, I am the first voice you hear. Oh, yeah, and that pain you get in your stomach over money, that's me, and it is a result of the fear I have instilled in you.

Is there any wonder why there has not been a transfer of wealth? In all of our lives we have submitted to this ruthless master called Mammon. Later in the book I am going to spend time uncovering even further this spirit so we can truly serve the only true God. I think it would be good for all of us to renew our vow to our Lord Jesus and repent for any attachment to Mammon.

Let us pray this prayer before we precede further, "Holy Father, we repent for being controlled by the voice of Mammon. Please forgive us and lead us to a deeper understanding of how our lives have been controlled though this spirit of greed and anti-Christ. Please restore us to your side and teach us to despise Mammon."

This prayer is only a beginning of our fight to become free from this demon. Our bondage to this devil did not begin yesterday. We have been conditioned all our life to trust in this filthy devil. It will require many battles and total reliance on the Holy Spirit to become free.

Continuing in Luke 16:14-15, we find some very interesting comments by Jesus,

> Now the Pharisees, who were lovers of money, also heard all these things, and they derided Him. And He said to them, "You are those who justify yourselves before men, but God knows your hearts. For what is highly esteemed among men is an abomination in the sight of God."

Jesus revealed plainly the heart of the Pharisees. These men tithed, gave offerings, were always in the synagogues and were the spiritual leaders of their day. These men were usually very wealthy, and Jesus made a statement then that might well be relevant today, "You justify yourselves before men."

As I mentioned earlier, some believe that material wealth among "Christians" somehow validates ones spiritual authority. I am not labeling all Christians who have wealth as Pharisees. I am saying that the rest of that Scripture is the bar by which we are all judged.

The motive for giving is of primary concern for our Lord and will be our determining factor as well. Scripture is rich with examples of how we are to prosper and not be in lack. That has not ever been disputed, but the "why we give" should always be judged.

This is usually the first level of giving, and if those who begin this way start to evaluate their motives and let the Holy Spirit deal with them, we will move to the next level of giving, which is giving out of obedience.

2. Giving From Obedience

This level of giving comes from listening to the voice of the Holy Spirit and developing a trust and confidence in Him. We have moved beyond trusting in Mammon and have repented from listening to that hateful anti-Christ voice. From this position of giving we start to understand that all we have and all we will ever have comes from our loving Father. He desires for us, His children, to be trained in the higher ways of stewardship. Therefore, He will test us in all levels of obedience and all levels of giving.

This type of giving is not to get, but to obey. Our true motive is to please the heart of the Father. The obeying in most cases is not easy, but we are learning to trust in something other than ourselves.

Once we enter this level of giving, the excitement of the Father to have found someone who trusts Him can be obvious. The Scripture in the beginning of Matthew Six says He will reward those openly who give to Him in secrete.

In my life I have experienced many situations in which my trust in God was tested. I can recall on one occasion the Holy Spirit prompted me to give a large sum of money to a ministry. The idea of giving several thousands of dollars on a credit card did not make sense to me. How many of us have learned that when the Lord speaks to give, the mind is not the instrument for arriving at a spiritual decision? We must simply obey regardless of what the rational mind says.

Fortunately, I overcame the voices of Mammon and fear to give what I heard the Lord say. Within a matter of hours after giving my offering, I was contacted by someone I did not know, to purchase equipment I had for sale. That sale more than made up for the offering.

I experienced a satisfying feeling of joy for having obeyed and a more exhilarating sensation for having pleased the Father. But beyond the feelings I had the sense that this act of obedience would produce a much greater return than mere reaping for having sown.

We have already spoken about one of the greatest acts of obedience demonstrated by Abraham. This was Abraham's willingness to sacrifice his son. This level of faith is not really understood today, although spoken about very often. Indeed the messages of faith are truly manifested in this example.

But what of the everyday people like you and me who have left everything at the altar to become true disciples of our Lord?

There are countless stories of precious saints who have witnessed in the spirit our Lord's suffering for their right to become an heir of salvation. Men like John G. Lake, who gave away his fortune to follow the call of God on his life. We all will have a choice to make at critical times in our lives. Will we be able to obey difficult instructions that in the visible realm seem perilous? Will we be able to walk in the supernatural realm to forsake the seen for the unseen?

Servants of God such as David, Joshua, Moses and others understood this high level of obedience. But the few of us "common folks" who have been instructed to give all we hold dear in this world must learn to consider what an honor and joy it is to be tested in this way.

This level of giving was tied to the observation made by the author of Hebrews 12:2 when he said "looking unto Jesus, the author and finisher of our faith, who for the joy that was set before Him endured the cross, despising the shame, and has sat down at the right hand of the throne of God"

We see an example of this giving, found in 1 Kings 17:10–14.

> So Elijah went to Zarephath. When he reached the town gate, he saw a widow gathering wood for a fire. Elijah asked her, "Would you bring me a little water in a cup so I may have a drink." As she was going to get his water, Elijah said, "Please bring me a piece of bread, too."
> The woman answered, "As surely as the Lord your God lives, I have no bread. I have only a handful of flour in a jar and only a little olive oil in a jug. I came here to gather some wood so I could go home and cook our last meal. My son and I will eat it and then die from hunger."
> "Don't worry," Elijah said to her. "Go home and cook your food as you have said. But first make a small loaf of bread from the flour you have, and bring it to me.

Then cook something for yourself and your son. The Lord, the God of Israel, says, 'That jar of flour will never be empty, and the jug will always have oil in it, until the day the Lord sends rain to the land.'"

We know that God usually spoke exclusively through His prophets in those days. And, until Peter received the revelation of who Jesus was, not many others who heard the voice of God were mentioned in the Scriptures. However, in the following text we see something extraordinary.

> Then the word of the Lord came to him, saying, "Go now to Zarephath, which belongs to Sidon, and live there; for I have commanded a widow there to feed you."
>
> *—1 Kings 17:8-9*

"God has commanded" is the part that stands out. I often wondered why God would speak to a non-Jew about providing food for His prophet. It occurred to me that God always had future generations on His mind. If He could not find Jewish people who would believe Him then He would find someone outside the covenant. Notice what Jesus said in the following scripture.

> Certainly there were many widows in Israel who needed help in Elijah's time, when there was no rain for three and a half years and hunger stalked the land. Yet Elijah was not sent to any of them. He was sent instead to a widow of Zarephath—a foreigner in the land of Sidon.
>
> *—Luke 4:25-26*

What was it about this woman that brought the riches of God to her house and family? There was something about the heart of this woman that captured the heart of the Father. I believe her level of honesty qualified her for one who would be obedient in giving all she had.

This woman says something interesting in verse 18 of 1 Kings 17 when her son dies. "Have you come to me to bring my sin to remembrance and to cause the death of my son". I believe this son was born out of wedlock. And the shame and guilt that this non-Jew had suffered created such a dialogue between her and God that the Father found someone He could trust.

Something happens to us when we find ourselves contrary to the God of the universe and facing certain death. We must make decisions from the heart hewed from honesty and recognition of our hopelessness without God. This woman found favor in the eyes of God. Not only was her provision being met but she was to witness the resurrection of her son.

The simplicity of truly believing, trusting in God, is the door to our greatest happiness. Unfortunately, many times we construct insurmountable walls created by doubt and unbelief that stop us from seeing great miracles.

I can also think of many situations in which I did not obey the voice of the Holy Spirit. I regret those decisions and I know that no excuse or rationalization justifies the disobedience. If only I had known then what I know now, I could have had major manifestations of His glory that would have saved many years of consequences for wrong decisions.

In the scriptures we find examples of disobedience that caused death and disasters. In Acts 4 and 5 we find an extraordinary account. Let us look at these verses and hear what the Holy Spirit is saying:

> Now the multitude of those who believed were of one heart and one soul; neither did anyone say that any of the things he possessed was his own, but they had all things in common.
>
> —*Acts 4:32*

When has the Church been of "one heart and one soul" since that time?

> And with great power the apostles gave witness to the resurrection of the Lord Jesus. And great grace was upon them all. Nor was there anyone among them who lacked; for all who were possessors of lands or houses sold them, and brought the proceeds of the things that were sold, and laid them at the apostles' feet; and they distributed to each as anyone had need. And Joses, who was also named Barnabas by the apostles (which is translated Son of Encouragement), a Levite of the country of Cyprus, having land, sold it, and brought the money and laid it at the apostles' feet.
>
> —*Acts 4:33-37*

We are seeing a great move of the apostolic in this hour, in some instances real, in some not. There is no question that the apostles of the early Church moved in the genuine. I believe the "real" move in this hour will be marked with great power and grace and there will be no doubt of which is which. The truth will speak for itself with signs and wonders causing resources to follow. There will be no need for creating programs and agendas fashioned after this world's system. God will never needed this world's system to support His agenda. We would all do well to consider these verses in Acts.

But a certain man named Ananias, with Sapphira his wife, sold a possession. And he kept back part of the proceeds, his wife also being aware of it, and brought a certain part and laid it at the apostles' feet. But Peter said, "Ananias, why has Satan filled your heart to lie to the Holy Spirit and keep back part of the price of the land for yourself? "While it remained, was it not your own? And after it was sold, was it not in your own control? Why have you conceived this thing in your heart? You have not lied to men but to God." Then Ananias, hearing these words, fell down and breathed his last. So great fear came upon all those who heard these things. And the young men arose and wrapped him up, carried him out, and buried him. Now it was about three hours later when his wife came in, not knowing what had happened. And Peter answered her, "Tell me whether you sold the land for so much?" She said, "Yes, for so much." Then Peter said to her, "How is it that you have agreed together to test the Spirit of the Lord? Look, the feet of those who have buried your husband are at the door, and they will carry you out." Then immediately she fell down at his feet and breathed her last. And the young men came in and found her dead, and carrying her out, buried her by her husband. So great fear came upon all the Church and upon all who heard these things.

—*Acts 5:1-11*

What would happen today if the Holy Ghost began to expose the hearts of givers? Would the term "slain in the spirit" take on a different meaning?

We must all fall on our face and ask mercy and forgiveness for wrong motives and disobedient hearts. The disobedient always cause harm not only to himself but to all that surround him or her.

I truly believe that when this apostolic age has matured, that we will begin to see the motives of our hearts revealed. We must all pray that we are ready and willing to be obedient to the voice of the Holy Spirit. Ultimately, when the time comes for our decisions to be made to obey or partially obey as Ananias and Sapphira did, what will each of us do?

The level of our giving must pass these tests in order to achieve the place of real intimacy with our Savior.

Doors will open when we pass our tests of giving. Our biggest door of resistance is when we refuse to look past our circumstances and rely on what the natural eyes can see. This only postpones the inevitable, the sacrifice of our self. This will require an all consuming love of commitment and realization of what has been accomplished for us through the cross. The passion of our Lord must consume each of us to take us to the next level of giving until we ourselves become the gift on the altar of self, called a living sacrifice by Paul in Romans 12.

3. Living Sacrifice

We are going to take a journey, beginning in the Old Testament with some examples of those who were living sacrifices. We have already spoken about Isaac. The interesting thing about Abraham's offering of obedience was that Isaac was just as obedient as his father. Isaac was at least a teenager and probably strong enough to have resisted if he had wanted. The fact that he did not makes the obedience two-fold, the giver and the gift. The analogy between Abraham and his son is the foreshadowing of the greatest love ever shown, Jesus, giving His life because of His love for His Father.

Now let us take a look at a living sacrifice who also knew how to give- Job 1:1-5.

> There was once a man in the land of Uz whose name was Job. That man was blameless and upright, one who feared God and turned away from evil. There

were born to him seven sons and three daughters. He had seven thousand sheep, three thousand camels, five hundred yoke of oxen, five hundred donkeys, and very many servants; so that this man was the greatest of all the people of the east. His sons used to go and hold feasts in one another's houses in turn; and they would send and invite their three sisters to eat and drink with them. And when the feast days had run their course, Job would send and sanctify them, and he would rise early in the morning and offer burnt offerings according to the number of them all; for Job said, It may be that my children have sinned, and cursed God in their hearts.

Most Bible historians agree that Job was perhaps, after Genesis one of the oldest books in the Bible. This means that long before Moses introduced the laws and customs associated with Judaism, Job already knew how to honor God with sacrifices. Job knew that hating evil and fearing God was a principle to live by, and doing it had always brought him riches and wisdom.

We will discover some important things about becoming a living sacrifice. The term sounds so holy and lofty. Yet, the price to become a living sacrifice is self evident. Job discovered that giving and being obedient positioned him so God could use a mortal man to give satan a foreshadow of his destiny.

One day the heavenly beings came to present themselves before the Lord, and Satan also came among them to present himself before the Lord. The Lord said to Satan, "Where have you come from?" Satan answered the Lord, "From going to and fro on the earth, and from walking up and down on it." The Lord said to Satan, "Have you considered my servant Job? There is no one like him on the earth, a blameless and upright man who fears God and turns away from evil. He still persists in his integrity, although you incited me against him, to destroy him for no reason." Then Satan answered the Lord, "Skin for skin! All that people have they will give to save their lives. But stretch out your hand now and touch his bone and his flesh, and he will curse you to your face." The Lord said to Satan, "Very well, he is in your power; only spare his life."

So Satan went out from the presence of the Lord, and inflicted loathsome sores on Job from the sole of his foot to the crown of his head. Job took a potsherd with which to scrape himself, and sat among the ashes.

Then his wife said to him, "Do you still persist in your integrity? Curse God, and die." But he said to her, "You speak as any foolish woman would speak. Shall we receive the good at the hand of God, and not receive the bad?" In all this Job did not sin with his lips.

—*Job 2:1-10*

Satan actually believed that Job was like most of us when threatened with losing our life, "skin for skin." This is where the tests of all tests begin in all of our lives.

If we ever reach this place of a living sacrifice, we must be prepared to become the bull on the altar and hopefully a pleasing fragrance to the Father.

The pain of losing everything, except a non-believing wife and three miserable comforters, must have been hell on earth for Job, yet despite all of this, the Bible says "Job sinned not. "

One of the lessons we can all learn from the experiences of Job is that all of us in our pursuit of God will be tested. These tests will measure just how much of our flesh and soul are in control of our decisions to "give our life."

We discover later that the soul is fragmented between the heart, mind and emotions. Giving tests the mind and heart of man. These areas were fragmented at the fall of Adam. Hebrews 4:12 talks about the word of God being sharp and powerful . . . " His word can cut through our spirits and souls and through our joints and marrow, until it discovers the desires and thoughts of our hearts."

Man is the only creature whose thoughts can differ from his intentions or motives. Jesus knew the heart of man and understood how to test the motives. **Giving is the one key that must unite motives and thoughts for our relationship to deepen.**

If our giving is corrupted by "what is in it for me?" attitudes, then we will never progress. If we want to pass the level of "giving to get" and move into the level of "giving out of obedience," then we must be sensitive to the precious Holy Spirit and His methods of testing.

Job did not know the way of the cross and yet he was willing through faith to trust God and retain his integrity. Job was a living sacrifice that produced such an aroma in the nostrils of God that Satan was shamed by a mortal man.

The pain of losing everything was bad enough, but the continual torment of the miserable comforters was and is today just like Satan. What joy the Father received when Job prayed for his tormenters after his trial. This would be like kicking the bruise already visible on the head of Satan.

Job's name is mentioned in Ezekiel 14:13-14 as one of three righteous men. The word of the Lord came again to me, saying: "Son of man, when a land sins against Me by persistent unfaithfulness, I will stretch out My hand against it; I will cut off its supply of bread, send famine on it, and cut off man and beast from it. "Even if these three men, Noah, Daniel, and Job, were in it, they would deliver only themselves by their righteousness," says the Lord God.

This speaks volumes of how pleased God was with this man's living sacrifice. Job was still on God's mind, long after he had died. This gift of Job's was counted as righteous. We all will have this opportunity to present our selves before the Lord as a living sacrifice.

The next example of a living sacrifice is found in Romans 12. We will describe in some detail what this phrase means:

I beseech you therefore, brethren, by the mercies of God, that you present your bodies a living sacrifice, holy, acceptable to God, which is your reasonable service. And do not be conformed to this world, but be transformed by the renewing of your mind, that you may prove what is that good and acceptable and perfect will of God.

The man who pinned that scripture knew something about becoming a living sacrifice. Paul had been a zealot for years before being introduced to the One he was persecuting on the road to Damascus.

Paul known as Saul was the tormentor used by Satan to harass and kill early believers. Saul believed it was his duty as a good Pharisee to uphold the Levitical Law of Moses and destroy all those who were followers of this blasphemer called Jesus. However, Jesus was able to transform the executioner into the deliverer. This transformation took place as a result of the death of Saul and the resurrection of Paul.

This can happen to us when we place our self on the altar. What is tied to the altar is not what rises from the altar.

But even though the spiritual transformation took place on the road to Damascus, I believe something even more dramatic happened in the spirit realm at Jerusalem when Saul watched Stephen being stoned.

Look at the following scripture in Acts 7:51-8:1, in which Stephen was preaching his last sermon.

You stiff-necked people, uncircumcised in heart and ears, you are forever opposing the Holy Spirit, just as your ancestors used to do. Which of the prophets did your ancestors not persecute? They killed those who foretold the coming of the Righteous One, and now you have become his betrayers and murderers. You are the ones that received the law as ordained by angels, and yet you have not kept it.

When they heard these things, they became enraged and ground their teeth at Stephen. But filled with the Holy Spirit, he gazed into heaven and saw the glory of God and Jesus standing at the right hand of God. "Look," he said, "I see the heavens opened and the Son of Man standing at the right hand of God!" But they covered their ears, and with a loud shout all rushed together against him. Then they dragged him out of the city and began to stone him; and the witnesses laid their coats at the feet of a young man named Saul. While they were stoning Stephen, he prayed, "Lord Jesus, receive my spirit." Then he knelt down and cried out in a loud voice, "Lord, do not hold this sin against them." When he had said this, he died. And Saul approved of their killing him.

I believe Stephen's prayer is what touched the heart of God and marked Saul to become Paul. That prayer, which can only be uttered from a place of "being full of the Holy Ghost," is an atomic bomb in the spirit. The love in those words will rip the veil from our spiritual eyes. This prayer is what comes from the heart of someone who has mastered the key of giving in all of its stages.

Please see the power that comes from someone who was truly a living sacrifice. Stephen's prayer produced such power in the heavens that Saul, who was not even aware of the spiritual significance of these words, was marked for the rest of his life.

The event on the road to Damascus was the physical manifestation of what had been accomplished in the spirit realm. **The blindness of Saul had been changed to produce the vision for Paul.** When the scales fell from the eyes of Saul the transplanted heart from Stephen to Paul had been completed. Those three days of blindness could never reveal the level of light that was filling the spirit of Paul. It was the mantle of Stephen being wrapped around the very soul of Paul. What the witnesses did in stoning Stephen by laying down his coat at the feet of Saul was a physical manifestation and spiritual act of the mantle being passed to him. What Paul says in Romans 1:14 express what took place in his life.

> I am a debtor both to Greeks and to barbarians, both to wise and to unwise. So, as much as is in me, I am ready to preach the gospel to you who are in Rome also.
>
> —*Romans 1:14-15*

For I am not ashamed of the gospel of Christ, for it is the power of God to salvation for everyone who believes, for the Jew first and also for the Greek. For in it the righteousness of God is revealed from faith to faith; as it is written, "The just shall live by faith."

—*Romans 1:16-17*

Paul became a debtor to Stephen to fulfill the life he, Saul eliminated. Is this not the position in which we all find ourselves? **If we can see that we all are debtors by the crucifixion of our Lord and Savior, we too will become a living sacrifice.**

We are talking about becoming the gift. Paul became the gift by presenting his body a living sacrifice. He knew that dead bodies were not acceptable, nor were the lame, blemished or any other defection. God gave His best and expects nothing less from us. We must come to the altar of God with our bodies as a living sacrifice.

When we have reached this point in our Christian giving, we have come to the altar of God, where obedience now changes to understanding. This is the purest form of giving. This is the example God's only son set. This must be the goal for the Church, whose purpose is to please the Father.

Once we become the gift, Abba knows we mean business with Him. This is not where or when we need to be concerned about the principal of sowing and reaping. This is when we come to understand "giving is better than receiving."

This is the condition where one lives by faith. This is the situation in which you can walk in the spirit and not the flesh. This is where all of us want to be.

This is where the renewal of the mind begins to manifest the will of the Father. This is the place where the true confessions we make of His promises begin to manifest in our lives.

This is where you and I can live, if we are willing to pay that price. That price is our life, as we know it now. This is why our minds must be transformed, because the life we presently understand is like looking through a dirty window. We can not see the complete picture or correct image. So what we see is incomplete; it has missing information that is critical for our understanding of each situation we encounter.

How many times in our life do we make decisions calculated on wrong images? Why is our image of the Father so different from person to person? I submit to you that our information is corrupted. Much like what happens to a computer, when the wrong data is entered; the wrong answer appears. The old adage "what you put in to something is what will come out."

If unchanged minds try to understand the Spirit, inevitably we will have the wrong perception of Him and this results in bad decisions and frustrated lives. However, if we go to the altar with everything we have, not just in money but our lives, then something is altered in our minds. That something will eventually affect our heart, which eventually will affect our souls.

Paul says work out your salvation with fear and trembling. Salvation is worked out when the mind is transformed. That transformation must begin in a new breed of believers who move past the "giving to get" attitude. This will release the people from the giving from obedience level to finally becoming the gift.

We as the Church must become this living sacrifice corporately. In doing so, we will introduce a whole new generation to a life in which the supernatural will become the natural way of living.

2
Prayer:
The Second Key

This chapter will change the way we pray. Read the follwoing verses in Matthew 6:5-15.

And when you pray, you shall not be like the hypocrites. For they love to pray standing in the synagogues and on the corners of the streets, that they may be seen by men. Assuredly, I say to you, they have their reward. But you, when you pray, go into your room, and when you have shut your door, pray to your Father who is in the secret place; and your Father who sees in secret will reward you openly. And when you pray, do not use vain repetitions as the heathen do. For they think that they will be heard for their many words. Therefore do not be like them. For your Father knows the things you have need of before you ask Him. In this manner, therefore, pray:

Our Father in heaven, Hallowed be Your name. Your kingdom come. Your will be done on earth as it is in heaven. Give us this day our daily bread. And forgive us our debts, As we forgive our debtors. And do not lead us into temptation, But deliver us from the evil one. For Yours is the kingdom and the power and the glory forever. Amen.

For if you forgive men their trespasses, your heavenly Father will also forgive you. But if you do not forgive men their trespasses, neither will your Father forgive your trespasses.

—*Matthew 6:5-15*

The next "key" Is prayer. Jesus showed us that order is important for unlocking doors. Once we learn to "become the gift" in giving we can be taught a new way to pray. A great majority of Christians are not motivated to pray, or if they do, they lack essential understanding to be effective.

This key of prayer is so significant to our development that it can only be placed in the hands of those who have mastered the key of giving.

Praying does to our mind what giving has accomplished in our heart. The heart which has been so corrupted by selfishness must be on the altar of God before the mind can be transformed by thoughts of the Father.

Our mind must be freed from thinking we must be the center of everything we do for God. It is in this "position" that the Lord can begin to show us how to pray.

The prayer of which I speak is nothing like what we have learned, or worse yet, how we imagine. True prayer is entering into the mind and heart of the Father to become His wishes on earth as it is in Heaven.

This understanding of prayer can only be given to the believer who has entered through the door of giving. The Lord is quick to reward those who follow His pattern of giving and then praying. We see throughout the chapter of Matthew 6 His response to our going in secret to meet Him.

The secret place is a special meeting area designed to be different each time so that man, as he so quickly does, will not make a religious ritual or sacred method of meeting God.

It is called the secret place because it is secret each and every time we meet with Him. The way to the Father must be different each time so He can continue to reveal to us the motives of our hearts.

Praying is one of the few things we can do in our Christian development that will always please the Father. Abba is our Father and likes to hear from His children.

Children are basically selfish and limited when it comes to conversation, but Abba has a way of training those who at least make an effort to speak to Him. So we must not be discouraged about our beginnings in our prayer lives.

I can recall in my early attempts at prayer becoming so frustrated because of the time that was spent in "vain repetitions." I hoped that my words were heard because I believed that was my right as a Christian. I honestly do not think any of my prayers were answered.

Looking back, I see the wisdom of God not to respond to those prayers, because most of those prayers were selfish and if answered could have made my life more hellish than it was already. You have heard from the secular world the phrase; "Be careful what you pray for as you may well receive what you ask" Even unbelievers understand the power of prayer.

Average Christians believes that prayer is the child telling the "Father" what he or she wants. Although the Father is very interested in hearing from His children, He is much more concerned about their motives. An exchange free of hidden agendas and self gratification is what receives the attention of our heavenly Father.

Imagery is terribly important in any relationship. It is because we lost ours in the Garden of Eden that the Father is eager to reform His image in us. The image we begin with in prayer must be changed. This takes time spent in His presence without the pursuit of anything other than Him.

There are several levels and positions of prayer:

Prayer Of The Mind

This type of praying is typical of the Christians who have not gone through the process of receiving the key of giving. These believers have not gone to the altar of self denial and thus do not know how to pray.

Prayers from the untransformed mind have little to no impact in the spirit realm. We have already learned that faith does not reside in the mind. This could be why the Holy Spirit is not received or understood by the majority of the people on the planet.

We are all trained to memorize, categorize and process through the mind and in order to make decisions. We are taught this procedure in most schools of elementary and secondary education. This training is considered to be the most important part of our development. The time and energy spent in developing the senses of the natural realm is staggering, particularly considering our average life span is around 70 years.

The real tragedy is that so few are aware of the spirit realm and even fewer know how to access it. Those who have understanding are usually not the Christians. It has been our experience that only small parts of the leadership are themselves capable of "moving in the spirit."

Moreover, we find that those who have knowledge of this realm are those in the New Age which is nothing more than old witchcraft redressed to appear refined and intellectually acceptable.

The prayers of the mind are those that do not originate from the Holy Spirit, but in the carnal souls of people.

These prayers create in the Christian a sense of well being. This is because man has always wanted religion to tell him how to act, what to do, what rules he must follow, etcetera. Religion takes the place of God and leaves man defenseless when it comes to dealing with devils and demonic influences.

We have to understand that prayer begins by living our lives in a particular way. Jesus explained this to His disciples, illustrating several important points. First and foremost Jesus said no man can be His disciple unless he is willing to leave everything.

> Whoever comes to me and does not hate father and mother, wife and children, brothers and sisters, yes, and even life itself, cannot be my disciple. Whoever does not carry the cross and follow me cannot be my disciple.
>
> —*Luke 14:26-27*

Comprehending this principle comes from the place of realizing your life is no longer your own. This should eliminate immediately of praying from our mind.

The one who prays from the mind is the one who thinks his prayers are heard from his much speaking. The mind is full of noise, primarily because it is the center of voices.

These voices are from the "master" we have chosen to listen to. In an earlier chapter we spoke about the voice of Mammon. Every voice other than the Holy Spirit is designed by the enemy to create fear and doubt.

So prayers coming from the mind that has not been reformed into the image of Christ will pray selfish and frightened prayers The reason for this is because the one praying is convinced by the enemy that his or her needs must be met for their well being to be maintained. The motive behind these prayers is fear, not faith. The mind, because of its very fallen nature, must believe that it is secure and protected in order to function properly.

It is easy to see why these prayers have no effect and rather produce false images of our Father. We have spoken earlier about the need for a new or transformed mind. This will be a theme through our study.

The unregenerate mind will lose every battle against the devil. There is no amount of praying of this kind that will protect you or will reveal information from the Father by the Holy Spirit. In fact, the natural mind will not allow you to understand the Bible at all. The Bible is written by the Spirit and which by necessity causes it only to be realized through our spirits.

Therefore, if our prayer life is empty and tedious, we would do well to follow the pattern set by Jesus. That pattern is to follow the Spirit. The Spirit will teach us how to give out of obedience before showing us how to pray.

Then let the Holy Ghost take us beyond "what we can even believe or understand." Then He will open a door of praying like we have never had before. Step by step each of us can increase our faith. Then we will not only increase our faith but rely totally upon the Holy Spirit for our "daily bread."

When we have entered through the door of prayer opened by the key of giving, we immediately begin to move past the mind and start to pray directly from our spirit.

Praying From The Spirit

This type of praying is recognizable by the evidence of many things, not the least of which is receiving answers to our prayers. Prayer becomes one of the most valuable substances of your daily life; because you are becoming one mind with the most awesome praying Spirit- the Holy Spirit.

"GIVE us this day our daily bread," this is an example that we must be a giver in order to ask to be given. And then notice how the food is wrapped in every day's revelation, which is our daily bread. Each day becomes food for our spirit because the Holy Spirit has plans for that day from before the foundation of the world, and to discover this becomes our sustenance.

We have already become a "living sacrifice" upon the altar of our God. We have developed that level of trust to believe our heavenly Father will take care of OUR every need, but what about His needs.

The Father is longing for children who will mature so that He can trust them as stewards of His Kingdom. This requires children who are willing to hear His spirit and begin to share in the obligations of a steward. Stewards must understand their duties. This is only possible by praying in and from the Spirit.

> For the Spirit searches all things, yes, the deep things of God. For what man knows the things of a man except the spirit of the man which is in him? Even so no one knows the things of God except the Spirit

of God. Now we have received, not the spirit of the world, but the Spirit who is from God, that we might know the things that have been freely given to us by God. These things we also speak, not in words which man's wisdom teaches but which the Holy Spirit teaches, comparing spiritual things with spiritual. But the natural man does not receive the things of the Spirit of God, for they are foolishness to him; nor can he know them, because they are spiritually discerned.

—1 Corinthians 2:10-14

Prayer is no longer our voice emanating from the fallen condition of our mind but the Spirit of God communicating with our spirit in a glorious exchange orchestrated from heaven and demonstrated on earth through a vessel yielded to the ways of the Spirit. This beautiful condition is where our duties as steward become realized. As we hear the Father's heart, our spirit is united to His in such compassion and faith that our very existence is altered.

When we find our self in this heavenly cooperation, our needs, such as food, shelter, money etc. become unimportant. After all, we are now participating with the Spirit of God in establishing His kingdom on earth. His Kingdom dominates every material substance in the universe. This is what Jesus demonstrated every time He changed water to wine or fed the multitudes or commanded a fish to swallow a gold coin.

These prayers are kingdom prayers designed to establish agreement for something much higher than our needs and wants.

> For we do not know what we should pray for as we ought, but the Spirit Himself makes intercession for us with groaning which cannot be uttered. Now He who searches the hearts knows what the mind of the Spirit is, because He makes intercession for the saints according to the will of God.
>
> —*Romans 8:26-27*

This passage from the Bible is generally quoted when someone is speaking about persons praying in unknown tongues. But have we ever considered that our precious Holy Spirit is so grieved by our conditions of "darkness" that He has no words to express His feelings to the Father? When we join our spirits with His, we too, have no earthly words that can express our conditions.

This position of prayer is from and in the Spirit. This is not a place in our minds and emotions.

God is a God of order and design and requires true Christians disciplined to join Him in prayers that unlock the destinies of peoples and countries. **Praying this way in the spirit demands such high level obedience and perseverance that without the key of giving one does not have the capacity to enter and believe for what the Holy Spirit will reveal.**

This not only requires praying in the spirit, but faith at the level of the Holy Spirit. That faith comes by hearing and hearing by the Word of God is a fact, but the truth of that verse becomes reality in this place of prayer.

Why? Because you will hear the Spirit of God and what you hear you believe and begin to speak. (Romans 10: 9-10) This creates the faith of God, through the Rhema word being heard and repeated. This is also the effectual prayer of the righteous man spoken of in James chapter 4.

Prayer must be an exchange of what is happening in Heaven with what is going on in the earth. If this does not take place, true prayer has not been experienced. Every thing that happens from the spirit realm is looking for an avenue to be manifested in the natural.

When Jesus said "I only do what I see my Father do," that was not something said to merely fill the pages of the Bible. This was a teaching to show us how to pray. Everything we need and everything the Father wants to manifest has already been done. Prayer is not just communication but demonstration.

> Jesus said to them, "Very truly, I tell you, the Son can do nothing on his own, but only what he sees the Father doing; for whatever the Father does, the Son does likewise. The Father loves the Son and shows him all that he himself is doing; and he will show him greater works than these, so that you will be astonished. Indeed, just as the Father raises the dead and gives them life, so also the Son gives life to whomever he wishes."
>
> —*John 5:19-21*

This statement was intended to show us that as we actually unite with the Holy Spirit we lose all of our own identity and become one voice. That voice has no fears, doubts, or unbelief. That voice calls things from heaven to earth and sees the end from the beginning. This is the voice that said "let there be light" and there was and it was good. Prayer has become the language of heaven. Let that sink deep into our spirit.

We are dealing with powers so great that our earthly bodies and minds are unable to comprehend the magnitude. That is why it requires the training Jesus is describing through Matthew 6.

Becoming The Prayer

The prayer above is an example in which Jesus did only what he saw the Father doing is a wonderful revelation of the level of prayer that changes things in the natural realm.

But you might say, that was Jesus, how can we see the Father? Jesus was trained by the Holy Spirit to enter such intimacy with the Father that seeing the spirit realm and watching His Father was His everyday life. That reproduced on earth what He saw in Heaven and was as natural to Him as breathing.

Praying at this level is not something anyone can understand without first becoming the gift and going through the "fire" Jesus wraps His people in.

John said, "I am just baptizing with water. But someone more powerful is going to come, and I am not good enough even to untie his sandals. He will baptize you with the Holy Spirit and with fire."

—*Luke 3:16*

We spoke earlier about praying in the "spirit," but "becoming the prayer" is a level beyond. We must become the fire from the altar of heaven. This is something very powerful! Let's consider it for a moment.

We began our prayer life by uniting with the Spirit of God. Gradually we began to see that the more the Holy Spirit controls our life the more fire burns within our spirits. The more the fire burns within us the less "chaff" remains. The fire becomes so intense that we are consumed and become the incense mentioned in Revelation and the coal on the altar of God spoken of in Isaiah.

After he had taken it, the four living creatures and the twenty-four elders knelt down before him. Each of them had a harp and a gold bowl full of incense, which are the prayers of God's people

—*Revelation 5:8*

Then one of the seraphim flew to me, having in his hand a live coal which he had taken with the tongs from the altar. And he touched my mouth with it, and said: "Behold, this has touched your lips; your iniquity is taken away, and your sin purged."

—*Isaiah 6:6-7*

When we become the "prayer" we are truly unrecognizable to ourselves. The Father, whose heart has always been to bring back His children, begins to pray through us. This manifests beyond groans into spiritual fire on the altar of God. This fire as it burns away our sins and iniquities becomes incense. The smell coincides with the amount of soul and flesh being burned. As we surrender more and more of our selves the aroma changes.

Finally, when there is only our renewed mind and soul on the altar the fragrance smells heavenly. This is the aroma that penetrates the hearts and minds of those to whom the Father has assigned our prayers.

This sweet aroma created by these prayers, sometimes called intercession, becomes a powerful weapon. These prayers contain all the properties of the Spirit. Our prayers there are atmosphere changing. So much so we are not sure if we are in the body or out.

> I know a man in Christ who fourteen years ago—whether in the body I do not know, or whether out of the body I do not know, God knows—such a one was caught up to the third heaven. And I know such a man—whether in the body or out of the body I do not know, God knows— how he was caught up into Paradise and heard inexpressible words, which it is not lawful for a man to utter.
>
> —*2 Corinthians 12:2-4*

Many great men of God attained this level of development in prayer. Jesus was the perfect example of them all.

The first prayer we will speak about that touched the heart of the Father was spoken by none other than our Lord and Savior Jesus.

> And when they had come to the place called Calvary, there they crucified Him, and the criminals, one on the right hand and the other on the left. Then Jesus said, "Father, forgive them, for they do not know what they do."
>
> —*Luke 23:33-34*

This prayer can only be prayed when we are full of the Holy Ghost. This prayer is the standard by which all other prayers must be judged. It's the sweet aroma, which is God himself manifesting in the sacrificial fire.

Prayer of this kind becomes like the spirit. It moves like the wind to change atmospheres, affect hearts and change the destinies of man. Jesus became the prayer of his Father, the very essence of His love, poured down for all mankind.

The prayers modeled by Jesus are so powerful that when spoken Heaven was already fulfilling the desire. He said:

> The truth is, anyone who believes in me will do the same works I have done, and even greater works, because I am going to be with the Father. You can ask for anything in my name, and I will do it, because the work of the Son brings glory to the Father. Yes, ask anything in my name, and I will do it."
>
> —*John 14:12-14*

Here we see the key to becoming the prayer. Jesus knew how much the Father desires to please His children. Jesus, through His obedience unto death became the answer for his Father. This gives his Father the honor and glory He desires and brings every angel to attention at the name of Jesus.

In the Father's eyes, ears and nostrils, He sees, hears, and smells our prayers. These prayers are measured by how much of Jesus we are filled with.

Let me explain it another way. Our souls are like an Old Testament altar, to which the sacrifices were brought by the high priests. The sacrifices are our thoughts; our habits, our imaginations, our images, our desires and dreams. When these are brought to the altar of our soul and burned, the fragrances, sounds, and sights that are emitted show the quality and quantity of our sacrifice.

This can reveal our level of giving and praying. If the aroma is sweet and the fire all – consuming, then whatever we ask the Father in Jesus' name will be done. The Father knows through the fragrance of our prayers, if they come from a vessel filled with the essence of His son.

The Father saw and heard the agony of His son in Gethsemane. The sight of blood coming from the pores in his body emitted an odor like no other. His odor was more than a body and soul dying. That odor came from a life of total surrender and total victory.

The prayer: from Gethsemane flowed from the heart of His Father who had already crowned Him above every-thing in heaven and on earth. Those are the prayers that the disciples learned about after the death and resurrection of Jesus. They learned those prayers in their own Gethsemane.

Gethsemane will be where each of us will learn as well. When Jesus said "take up your cross and follow me," he was speaking about going through "the garden" to pick up our own cross.

These prayers are not something most Bible schools teach, or can they be learned from theories. These type of prayers come from the spirit of God through vessels emptied of themselves and not concerned with self preservation. We all must evaluate our life and where we are in the development of our prayer life. Then decide where we would like to be and how to arrive. This honest appraisal will hopefully lead us, to make quality decisions concerning this most important issue in our Christian walk.

I can remember one day not long ago when something extraordinary happened to me and my wife. We were in our prayer room early one morning, which is our practice when we are at home. Our prayer room is one of the nicest rooms in our home. In fact we decided to make our dining room the ministry office so we could turn one of the bedrooms into our prayer room. This has become one of the most precious places in our home.

One morning as we entered into the room and sat down to worship the absolute Glory of God descended. The weight of His Glory was so intense we could not move. We were caught up into this ecstasy every morning for almost a month. During these days, we would talk to Him and ask Him things, but He never responded.

We were somewhat concerned because so often during our worship the Lord reveals powerful life-changing truths for our lives. So, being human, we were wondering if we had offended our sweet Holy Spirit. But that did not seem to be the case, since His presence was so strong in that room. Finally, the Lord began to reveal to us that He was not angry or offended with us. But in fact, He had found a place where He could come and feel the Love and Peace He, Himself was bringing. He had just wanted to come and Rest. We were speechless and so honored to have provided a place for the King of Glory to rest His Head. Alleluia!

It is the Holy Spirit's desire that we all begin to understand the journey which lies beyond us. I believe Jesus gave us valuable keys to unlock doors that hold these mysteries and so much more.

I know that giving unlocks the door so we might learn how to pray. Then, through His grace we can move step by step to discover what was hidden. The process of prayer development is in direct proportion to our process of self-denial.

There is nothing more critical for us to understand than that what and where we are now is a direct result of whom we are serving. This is expressed in every aspect of our life, but most profoundly in our giving and praying. Our location in Christian maturity does not depend solely on Jesus or the Holy Spirit, but our choices as well.

We made the choices and paid the price to arrive where we are now. Now we must pay the price to leave where we are at present, in order to seize the prize that is set before us.

The price we must pay to get that prize is not as great as the reward or nearly as costly as the alternative. Choosing our own ways, or the good ideas of this world is much more costly than we think, with no eternal fruit at the end. We all must come to the realization on this journey that there is no escape from this life alive.

Many people live their lives, as if there was not death at the end of this natural existence. They prefer to live in a fantasy world, in which they go through life in absolute denial. Most choose not to even think of an end to a life filled with "their make-believe existence." However, not thinking about it will not make it less a reality, nor will filling up your life with material wealth create an alternative.

There is a spirit realm that dominates the natural. The sooner we qualify for authority in that kingdom the better. We can either be co-dominators with the Holy Spirit in that realm or be dominated by the devil and our unreformed minds and hearts.

The qualification is measured, at first, by the level of our giving and praying. Our abilities are then determined by the keys we acquire and the doors we enter. God will never force man to do anything he does not choose.

I know there are more than three levels in any topic Jesus discussed in Matthew 6. I have observed that just as giving transforms the mind and heart, praying intensifies that work and in addition begins to reform the soul.

In order for our soul to be totally reformed, the flesh must be dominated by the Spirit.

As we progress through the revelations of giving and prayer, we begin to realize that our flesh must undergo the transformation process released through fasting.

So an additional key is given to our understanding as a result of our prayer life. That key unlocks a door that has not only been locked but difficult to even approach for most Christians, and that is fasting.

Let us take the key of prayer and unlock the door of fasting. We will discover why it is sequenced in Matthew 6 and how our lives can become lethal to the enemy with this revelation.

3
Hungry For Fasting

In the preceding chapters I developed levels of giving and then did the same with prayer. As I said before, I know there are many levels of both giving and praying. It is my intention to illustrate them to challenge and encourage the body of Christ. I have no desire to make a dogma or religion. These different plateaus are purely subjective and are from my personal experiences and revelations. They have tremendously enriched my life and that is why I want you to have them.

The truth is, in our natural man, we are all limited by our experiences and mental capacities at any given time in our life's journey.

One of the sweetest things about our precious Holy Spirit is He uses our limited understanding, where we are, and begins to reveal life changing truths from His Word. These truths, although always having been available, enlighten our understanding in the exact season of our greatest needs. Then, immediately we are propelled into a dimension filled with faith and passion. This is such a beautiful picture of why the Bible is a spirit book and can never be understood by anything other than a spirit being. The Holy Spirit then reveals more Truth from that new place. This place is far more accessible to His spirit than where our dull unenlightened souls had been. We all know who the person of Truth is: In John 14:6 Jesus declares **"I am the way, the truth and the life."** This is what happens each time we are given a "key" to the next door, we discover more of the way, the truth, and the life of our Master.

Having said that, we will now explore the next part of Mathew 6:16–18:

> And now about fasting, when you fast, declining your food for a spiritual purpose, don't do it publicly, as the hypocrites do, who try to look wan and disheveled so people will feel sorry for them. Truly, that is the only reward they will ever get. But when you fast, put on festive clothing, so that no one will suspect you are hungry, except your Father who knows every secret. And he will reward you.

Most of us have attempted fasting at one time or another in our life. Too often, it becomes retched experiences; we spent more time thinking about food than anything else. What we were trying to sacrifice became our obsession.

The Church has become a group in which most of its members are overweight and unhealthy from overeating, or consuming the wrong type of food. In fact, if any one group on earth should be fasting, it is the Church.

It seems most events sponsored by the Churches are held in conjunction with dinners and breakfasts. This is not evil or wrong by any means, but does send signals that gluttony is less a sin than others.

Fasting seems to be one of those words not spoken about often in Church so as not to offend the overweight crowd. Or, if it is mentioned, it is usually spoken light heartedly, followed by nervous laughter.

In Jesus' days the Pharisees were champion fasters and they let everyone know it. In fact, they gave, prayed, and fasted more than probably the average Christian does today. So obviously giving, praying, and fasting does not imply that our behavior is acceptable to God.

Everything the Pharisees were doing: giving, praying and fasting were commanded by God. **The problem was not what they did but the false motives in their hearts.**

If the hearts of Christians today are not changed, we will have the same religious structure Jesus is speaking about. In fact, if we take an objective look, we see the same problems in the Church as in so-called "heathen" society.

The Church has lost power to appeal to the world because it offers little if any real spiritual values, not because of what is said, but because of what is done.

So, in order to attract people, some churches resort to the system the world uses- entertainment, advertisement, "user friendly" environments, so not to offend visitors. These Church leaders want to offer programs and environments that make the "lost" or heathen feel accepted. This sounds appealing on the surface, but like everything else that comes from the "world system," it is false.

Remember when Satan told Jesus "If you would worship me, I would give you all the kingdoms of this world." He was offering Him, not only the nations but "The world's ruling system." I believe we can make the same analogy today. What he is now saying is: "If you worship me, following my world system, I will give you the multitudes. "It is not just about gathering crowds, but taking them to a real encounter with the Lord, that will turn them from sin and flesh which is "the world system, to the Kingdom of God.

One of the famous statements of the world is "The end justifies the means." This is far from being godly. The Father **does** care a lot about the means. Because worldly appealing, non-confronting, non-transforming methods can never lead to holy, righteous living.

I think every pastor would agree if you want to attract crowds you must invite Jesus as King and Lord first and allow Him to direct the activities. The transformation must begin within our minds and hearts as **the blueprints the Master designed.**

If we don't give, we can't expect to learn how to pray effectively. All this is so basic and yet so difficult for the Church to embrace.

The reason we are talking about this in our section of fasting is that most Churches are in a condition in which fasting would change their atmosphere dramatically. The pastors would not be spending night and day counseling their sheep. Instead, they would have more time to be with the Lord. But because many Church leaders, who themselves have never progressed from giving and praying cannot possibly understand fasting.

Fasting would bring the flesh under total subjection and the Churches today need this desperately. But there is a sequence and order in God.

When He showed Moses the tabernacle, He did so from the inside out. The design was first "The Holy of Holies," then "The Holy place," then "The Inner Court and then "The Outer Court." This is also the method God uses to change us, from the inside out.

Therefore, once our hearts and minds are transformed, we can begin with the flesh in our bodies. That is why fasting is sequenced the way it is in Matthew 6.

We are talking about fasting in this chapter, so to understand that in order to fast we must enter in through the proper door.

Remember what Jesus said in John 10? He was saying that those who try to gather the sheep by any means other than by Him are thieves and robbers. He said later in that chapter that He is the door by which sheep enter.

All of our programs and systems that have been devised by means other than God's ways are like the illustration above and will create problems, not solutions.

If we call for a forty day fast and pastor a Church that has less than 10% who tithe, what is the likelihood the fast will be successful? The same is true when we have all night prayer meetings or anything else requiring our hearts and mind to be controlled by the Holy Spirit.

We all know Jesus said to "love God with all our heart." Mark 12:30:

> And you shall love the Lord your God with all your heart, with all your soul, with your entire mind, and with all your strength.

So how can we possibly love God with all our heart, soul, and mind when we don't give or pray and much less fast? We have no understanding of the power required for that passage to be fulfilled.

This is the purpose of the revelations that the Holy Spirit is pouring out on earth in these last days. He knows the Church is in great turmoil. He knows we desperately need an "upper room" experience. So He is giving us keys to unlock life-changing, world shaking revelations that will expose and destroy this world's system.

Remember, revelation sometimes requires demonstration to become an impartation. In other words, we must use our physical bodies to perform an act associated with the revelation.

For example, Noah built an ark, Abraham was willing to sacrifice his son and Joshua marched around Jericho. These acts caused the revelation to become one with their spirit, and opened doors for the spirit realm and natural realm to interface. This is why our reformed hearts and minds require a physically submitted body. Our physical acts manifest the passion generated in our reformed souls by fasting.

A body can be used by God as a channel between the invisible and the natural realms. Daniel's diet and his fasting lifestyle contributed to the clear and powerful revelations that he experienced. The same is true with Elijah and John the Baptist. Our fasting results in impartations of revelation from the precious Holy Spirit.

When through our giving and praying we have demonstrated an understanding of trust and submission to the Father, then we are permitted access to a heavenly power that can deliver nations.

Jesus said in Matthew 17:14 and Mark 9:29, when speaking about delivering a boy, whom His disciples could not deliver, "This kind does not come out unless one has prayed and fasted."

Jesus was demonstrating and declaring the order of power for "kingdom manifestations." Prayer as we have discussed opens the door to fasting. Jesus followed the dynamics because He followed His Father's order. This divine pattern positioned Jesus in awesome places of authority for major deliverance.

That boy was not delivered because Jesus spoke, but it was from the position where Jesus spoke. If we can see the design of God we can see the weakness of our enemy. The design outlined by

Jesus in Matthew 6 is our road map to reformation and keys to operate in kingdom authority.

Transformation is the one essential ingredient that has been missing for us to live in the spirit as Paul described in Romans 8. This ingredient will take us back to the cross where our bodies must hang.

Fasting makes this a reality. If our bodies are on the cross our perspective and opinions change. "The spirit is willing but the flesh is weak," will not be heard from the cross. The place of power and transformation can be realized only from that position.

If only the Church will find that message again, the need for "programs" to attract crowds will diminish. Fasting is the single greatest weapon in the hands of the Christian that will cause hell to tremble and devils to flee.

If our Christian life is powerless and unsatisfying, it is because we have not allowed ourselves exposure to the spirit realm through the cross of His majesty. It is for such people that I want to say the following:

God has given everything to enable us to discover the wonders of His ways. He will not try to entertain you with tricks and gimmicks for your amusements and "lukewarm" attitudes. If you have ears to hear and eyes to see, He will transform your mediocrity into a life beyond what you or Hollywood could imagine.

I reached that point in my Christian life in which I made a choice to find God or die trying. I had my fill of the parlor tricks of the new age and the pseudo "Christian" life. I say pseudo because it had all the right languages and "acts" of power Christian living without any of the lasting fruit.

So I began to study the Scriptures with prayer and fasting. I accidentally discovered the design of God revealed in Matthew 6. The following was how I attempted to fast in the beginning. It also demonstrates the mercy of our God.

My experience with fasting began several years ago, even before I began to understand the process outlined in Matthew. I began to fast to eliminate toxins from my body. I had read that it was a good thing for the body to cleanse itself from the inside out. So I determined to begin a three day fast on liquids. My experience was probably very normal. I watched the clock and could not believe there were only 24 hours in a day. The three days finally ended and I had accomplished a measure of the detoxification that I had sought. But during those three days the Holy Spirit began to speak to me about some things in my life. He began to tell me that I was a slave to my mind and body and that He had not created me to live that way. He went on to describe how He would transform my thought process if I would submit to Him.

I had been praying the prayer in Ephesians 1:17–20 about having the spirit of wisdom and the eyes of my understanding opened. So I eagerly submitted.

The next morning He awoke me with a determination to fast like never before. I believed for seven days. I did not begin that day but planned to start the following week. Those of you who have scheduled something from God to begin at a certain date know the tactics of the enemy. Everything that could go wrong did. Machinery broke, my son misbehaved and I got sick. Nevertheless, I was determined to keep my appointment with the Holy Ghost.

My mind was busy sending all kinds of fear messages to my body. My body was reacting by sneezing, coughing and complaining. But, I remained resolute to break the chains of slavery over my life, and I began the seven day fast.

By the end of the third day my body was not hungry. By the fourth day I was feeling fresh and alive. I began to pray with a new energy and faith. When the fifth day arrived my spirit was receiving information from the Holy Spirit on Scriptures I had read and not understood for years.

As the days went on His presence grew until I began to weep uncontrollably. I was in the presence of the One my heart was seeking. I had felt His presence before, on a number of occasions. But this was different. It was as if He had decided to bring such a level of glory into my room that all I could do was see my wretchedness. The light and glory was so overwhelming that at times I could not rise off the floor.

I began to worship and express my grateful heart any way I could. I did not want to lose this indescribable feeling. During this time I was changing into something I did not know or understand. My desire to please the Father increased beyond my need to be blessed. I always had wanted to please Him but my thoughts and emotions had contaminated those efforts. I could not see Him in the absolute splendor of His majesty. The images created from my mind and heart had perverted His Holiness and Glory.

Suddenly, I could see the condition of my soul and body. I saw the chains of fear, sin and iniquity in my life. I began to hear the voice of the Holy Spirit directing me through worship on how to destroy those strongholds. As I began to shout and dance before the Lord, angels began to enter the room with swords like I had never seen before. They cut away a lot of the chains. Some of the things they did I had no understanding of then or even to this day. All I know is that the level of ecstasy I was experiencing was beyond description.

For some incredible reason, fasting had broken a hole in the barrier created by my wrong thoughts and images. It was like I saw for the first time images coming from heaven instead of my poisoned mind. The overwhelming sensations I experienced can not be done justice by words. Suffice it to say that the multidimensional facets of His majesty left me helpless to express anything but uncontrollable crying and joy.

My life was forever altered in that instant. In His mercy He opened the spirit realm for me to see. He began to tell me that fasting is a weapon the Church has avoided because of the lies of the enemy. He said He is going to use people like me to restore what had been stolen.

Since that time I have been on several fasts at the Lord's direction, some times over two hundred days in a year. The first forty day fast was a landmark in my Christian development. It was during that time that He revealed to me what I am sharing now.

Remember earlier when we spoke about the Pharisees being very diligent about fasting? In Luke 5:33-35 Jesus responds to the disciples of John the Baptist who wants to know why Jesus disciples do not fast. The answer given by Jesus is the heart and soul of fasting. He said, "Can you make the children of the bride chamber fast, while the bridegroom is with them?" Then He said, "But the days will come, when the bridegroom will be taken away from them, and then shall they fast in those days."

The more I have fasted the more I have longed for my bridegroom to appear. The words "in those days" could not have been more prophetic for the Church. We are living in the day in which our every action must demonstrate our total dependence upon the One to whom our hearts belong.

I recall once when I was fasting hearing the voice of the Holy Spirit asking me how much I desired the return of the only true King of Kings? I was puzzled by the question and asked Him why He was asking me this question. He proceeded to tell me that most of the Church today was more interested in their kingdom instead of His kingdom and that if the Church would cry out for His return like the children of Israel cried for a deliverer in Egypt that heaven would hear.

I have had such wonderful experiences in my times of fasting with the Lord that have changed my ways of thinking and believing. My life is truly no longer mine to do as I please. The most poignant understanding I have had through fasting is the realization that what Jesus did for me can not now or ever be repaid. This one truth has made me determined to lay my life down for Him at any price.

It is my desire that all of you who desire to enter into those places of intimacy with the Holy Spirit through fasting will find the courage and faith to begin your life of fasting for the bridegroom's return. Once you make the decision to begin you will never regret it.

One of the many beautiful things about the Holy Spirit is that He forgets your failures in the journey and capitalizes on your successes.

Our mind is the enemy of our spirit when the Holy Spirit is not in control. There will not be too many things in our life more difficult to achieve than fasting. This is exactly why the Holy Spirit is giving us keys.

Remember, the first key is the level of your giving. Have you become the gift? This will unlock the mystery of prayer. When you can become the incense on the altar of God, through your prayer life the next key is handed to you.

Always remember this journey we are taking is progressive. Each step requires more intense time with Him than before. This is to insure we do nothing routine or familiar as to elicit a certain response from the Holy Spirit. The secret place is called "secret" because it is such each time we seek to enter. Every fast is different and requires a new degree of sacrifice to destroy any preconceived routine or result.

The places the Holy Spirit wants to take each of us willing to submit will require total surrender. These are places in the spirit where love and truth reign supreme and the mind has no influence. This is the place the devil fears you're attaining and the place where angels are at your command. You were made before the creation of the world for this position in the heavenly realm.

I recall during one of my fasts that the Lord started to reveal to me how our images have been formed. He showed me that our senses have been poisoned by wrong eating, seeing and hearing, thus altering the chemicals in our bodies.

These chemicals actually work to form the thoughts and images in our brains. Once these thoughts are damaged, the images are also corrupted. If we continue to see the same corrupted images over and over, we begin to believe they are true. Whatever we continually hear we will believe, and whatever we continually see we will move toward and imitate.

Our minds play images in full stereo, so not only are we seeing something; we are hearing the dialogue of fear as well. These images are one of the primary influences by which we make choices in our lives.

These images also produce feelings of comfort or pain. And, eventually over time, our senses and emotions are so damaged that we need more and more stimulation to have any feelings. This is why

we are a society of gluttons, not only in foods but violence and every other form of self gratifications.

Man has always lived by the old saying, "If it feels good, do it." We begin to trust all the wrong images and thoughts created by wrong eating, wrong listening, and wrong viewing. The more we engage in these types of behavior the easier it is for us to believe the lies of the enemy. The easier it is for us to be controlled by fear. And the more difficult it is to hear anything from the Holy Spirit.

The Lord has shown me that fasting brings our body under submission. But what the Holy Spirit is ultimately after is bringing our thoughts into order. As the Apostle Paul said:

> For the weapons of our warfare are not carnal, but mighty through God to the pulling down of strong holds; casting down imaginations, and every high thing that exalteth itself against the knowledge of God, and bringing into captivity every thought to the obedience of Christ.
>
> —*2 Corinthians 10:4-5*

Fasting has many stages of development. One of those is our being consumed by the thoughts of God. Changing our thoughts requires seeing and hearing different images.

One way this is done is by removing the current source of the stimulation and replacing it with another. So taking away our current food source starts to clean the mind of wrong images. This is how I began and I think it can be useful for anyone serious about fasting.

When we begin to forfeit food to spend more time with the Holy Spirit, our distractions are diminished. This does not happen immediately, but as a result of learning how to give and pray, our success is faster. The activities of our thoughts slow down for us to carefully observe what is taking place in and around us. As this happens we start to observe strange phenomena.

Most of our thoughts are centered on only one or two themes. Usually, we become consumed with some form of self preservation and personal security. These themes are almost always connected with money in some form or other. This is a recurring thought even if it is disguised in different forms.

For example, when we are encouraged to "sow" into the kingdom of God, the immediate thought preceding giving is what will I reap? This is obvious; we spoke earlier about this problem in the body of Christ. **But what is not so obvious is our subtle way of saying, "We are not of this world" as a Christian Mantra, but making decisions that are designed as though we are building our kingdom on earth.**

For example, some years ago we were moving from one millennium to the next. The body of Christ was filled with warnings of disaster concerning the infamous Y2K. I found myself being encouraged or even warned by large ministries to buy gold and store food for the looming disaster. This was coming from a group of people who purported to have no ties with this world or its system.

For those who live according to the flesh set their minds on the things of the flesh, but those who live according to the Spirit set their minds on the things of the Spirit. To set the mind on the flesh is death, but to set the mind on the Spirit is life and peace. For this reason the mind that is set on the flesh is hostile to God; it does not submit to God's law—indeed it cannot, and those who are in the flesh cannot please God.

—*Romans 8:5-8*

This is the major strategy of the enemy. The enemy knows that in the flesh and the arena of the mind, he is the master of illusions. So he controls us with fear and pain which totally close our spirits. The images of fear have been rehearsed and "acted out" in our minds for years. So much so that our hearts contain layers of scar tissue protecting it from pain and rejection.

The heart is turned to stone and our minds are filled with images of failures, mistrust, and despair. So the minute we attempt to leave the natural realm and move to the spirit, our minds become filled with distractions. If we can be distracted by the illusion of solving our problems in our unreformed minds and cold harded hearts, our outcome is failure and our threat to the devil and his kingdom has been neutralized.

Can you see the genius of Jesus laying out this design in Matthew 6? He knows the power structure of the enemy, so He knows how to dismantle it as well. Remember, **If we**

can see the design of God, we can see the weakness of our enemy. This is why you will be hearing the word reformation from the bride of Christ in the days ahead.

As I said fasting has several stages of development in each one of us. The progress of our development is directly proportionate to our levels of giving and prayer. I am continually amazed how the Holy Spirit will take me deeper into His spirit through fasting, after I have just obeyed His instructions of giving or interceding.

Our giving to God begins to destroy our soul's hold over us through the fear of loss, greed or lust for power. The purpose of this battle is for our heart. This is where fear resides and builds walls for protection from the pain of past failures. We have all been conditioned to believe that if we have money, we will be secure, safe and pain free. And if we do not have money we believe the images and thoughts of destitution and fear created from society and our "friends".

These are the images that arise from a heart and mind that have not been transformed into His mind. These structures begin to fall when our hearts are reformed into the image of the One who bought and paid for us. **He paid a price we could never afford for a future we certainly do not deserve.** That is why He is so determined for us to see all that is ours through the cross.

Next, Jesus shows us how to pray, which again engages our soul. The soul is the battleground for all our emotions, images, and choices. Our minds are at the forefront in this battle because we like our comfort and have been told "seeing is believing." But we know that believing what we can not see is the first step to seeing in the spirit realm. This is why faith is never found in our minds.

Our mind requires proof from the natural realm before it will believe. The sad thing about this scenario is that most of the images our mind has been shown are created from illusion. **The devil has created false images conditioned by the fears he has tormented us with, to fool us into believing that what we are seeing in our minds is real.**

This is why prayer requires destroying more of the established structures. Prayer changes our mind by focusing on heavenly images that have broken through fear and doubt. The battle rages within us until something begins to change.

The change began from our encounter with giving that allowed light to transform our hearts. These changes are to eliminate some of the poisons those years and years of conditioning have produced.

Jesus knows the hearts and minds of man. He knows what must be done to reform man the image of the Father that was lost in the garden, must be reformed. His methods are perfect

Now we are introduced to fasting, the place where the body really begins to squirm. The body has been demanding its way for years. Now you are making the body do without its pleasures and comforts. No food, are you kidding? Think of it, the entire structure of the devil to control our every thought is under attack.

It is important to note that the process is never the same for each person. The only thing that is constant is the importance of dismantling the strongholds. Jesus our master designed this three-pronged attack to destroy the work of the devil in our lives.

The soul must be free in order for us to become the ultimate weapon against the devil. Remember when Jesus said in John 14:30 that the "prince of this world comes but has nothing in me." This is the condition of total victory, total authority, and complete dependence on the King of Kings. This is something you and I can achieve. The method is perfect and it will work if we are willing to begin where we are.

Before we move to the next part of Matthew, I would like to show an example from the scripture of these three keys in operation. Let's look in Acts 10:30–32:

> And Cornelius said: "Four days ago I was fasting until this hour; and at the ninth hour I prayed in my house, and behold, a man stood before me in bright clothing, and said, 'Cornelius, your prayer has been heard, and your alms are remembered in the sight of God. Send therefore to Joppa and call Simon here, whose surname is Peter.'"

This is the story of how a religious apostle met a spiritual heathen. How the heart of God was moved by giving, praying and fasting regardless of the race of Cornelius. The power of this man Cornelius was demonstrated in every aspect of his soul.

These are the characteristics that will cause Heaven to open for us as it did him. What is so remarkable about this account is how we see the operation of Matthew 6 releasing the power of the Holy Ghost. The soul of this man had been transformed long before Peter laid hands on him.

The giving and praying of this man had taken him to a dimension in the spirit realm perpetuated by his fasting. This is such a beautiful illustration of how to dismantle every religious structure and image of our hearts and minds.

Cornelius, I believe, hastened the release of the Holy Spirit to the gentiles. The amazing thing about the Holy Ghost is that He will respond to anyone who responds to His ways and methods.

We must remember that one of the primary goals of the Father is to destroy the evil that was released in the Garden of Eden. The image of God was destroyed, and the image of the devil was imprinted on our souls.

So when God can find someone who is willing to give at His leading, He will instruct the Holy Spirit to teach that person how to pray. This is what took place with Cornelius.

Then while Cornelius was fasting, the scripture says about the third hour he saw a vision. The number three through out the Bible speaks of the Godhead as well as completeness. I believe this was a sign to this "heathen" that he was being made whole, spirit, soul, and body, through his obedience and thirst after God.

This illustration speaks volumes to me about how much we can trust our Father with our very lives. It does not matter what anyone or any religion says about Jesus. It only matters that our hearts and minds are transformed so that we can receive directly from the source.

But the source, the Holy Spirit, can not send us images or sounds through a corrupted, unreformed receptor such as our minds and hearts. So He shows us how to clean our receptor, then He begins to educate us for higher responsibilities in His kingdom.

Cornelius was not only a high ranking officer in the natural army but was immediately promoted in the kingdom of God. His life caused the religious crowd to submit to the power of the Holy Ghost. What an awesome New Testament example of the power structure contained in Matthew 6 and the faithfulness of our Lord.

In closing our subject on fasting, I want to share a few observations that have been exposed to me at different times of fasting.

One such observation is how closely fasting and death resemble each other. I have never been close to physical death through fasting. Fasts of forty days are not life threatening, particularly if we consume plenty of liquids.

But when I thought of Moses fasting 80 days consecutively without water or food, I started to see how meager my fasts have been. I am also convinced that if we really want to move into the arena of the spirit realm, fasting and death overlap.

The term fasting has a sanitary spiritual connotation that is lost when we take the step that Moses took. In Moses' mind he was already face to face with his creator, so what difference did it make to him if his heart was beating?

Survival was only if he was interested in this planet. What he was witnessing was beyond what the natural realm could offer. Fasting or whatever Moses was experiencing was a by-product of the transformation process taking place.

Imagine with me if you will, Moses standing inside the cloud of God where there is no time, where the light from God's glory changed Moses very DNA. In fact it was so profound I think that is why Satan wanted his body. The transformation changed something in the chemical make-up of Moses, to the point that he could have lived, I believe like those of Adam's generation.

This body held secrets that God had buried in the flood to keep Satan from obtaining them. This hidden knowledge in the hands of demon possessed people such as Hitler; Hussein and future anti-Christ's could change the destiny of some nations and peoples.

God showed Moses every detail of the tabernacle in its splendor and grand design. This design was more than a tabernacle; it was God revealing to His servant His very nature.

Do you think we could become so immersed in the Glory of God that all of our necessities would be supernaturally supplied?

We have already spoken about the process of reformation that must begin from the heart of man progressing outward to the physical body. This is ultimately where the "rapture" will take place as far as I am concerned. That is not main stream theology but it is something to consider.

My fasts have been frequent and life changing but not even close to where the Lord is calling us. I believe that He wants all of us to walk with Him like Enoch and become a friend like Abraham.

In one of my fasts I awoke in the spirit to see angels bringing me food. I awoke so refreshed and filled that I did physical labor for several hours that day. This food, for lack of a better description looked like liquid light. The taste was indiscernible but I remember having the sensation of satiation.

I asked the Holy Spirit about that experience and He reminded me of what Jesus told his disciples when they returned to feed Him at the well in Samaria:

My food is to do the will of Him who sent Me, and to finish His work.

—*John 4:34*

My fasting has taken me to depths of my human condition that frightened me and strengthened my resolve at the same time. I saw that my life on this planet had no purpose apart from that of the Holy Ghost.

The greatest illusion perpetrated on all of us is to believe we can escape this life alive, in terms of our natural existence. As crazy as that sounds it is still the driving force behind most of our lukewarm attitudes.

I say lukewarm because we have not closed the door on our belief that "maybe this Christianity thing won't work." We have not totally sold out because we have one eye on the world and the other one on the hypocrisy in the Church.

So we rationalize that if we only have one life to live we better get all we can out of this world. Then our time on this planet is motivated by trying to satiate the present life and making some death bed confession of Christ before we die.

The fear of death becomes one of the most powerful weapons wielded by the enemy. However, if we follow the Holy Spirit in the depths of fasting through the method of our master, the enemy sees that the fear of death no longer holds us captive.

Fear starts to lose its grip in our life and we are ready for experiences with the Holy Ghost that we have only read about in the Bible. Our life will become a weapon in the hands of God that is fearless in the spirit realm.

Our attitudes of those around us will change. The life we are now living begins to transform right before our eyes, eyes that have become enlightened with the truth of who we are in Christ.

This level of faith creates boldness in us to transform the dying world around us. The transformation I am speaking of will not come from predigested sermons and seminaries.

This will take place from a reformed person radiating the love of Christ and the power of the cross simultaneously.

The fear that once spoke to us on a consistent basis loses its influence over our decisions. The questions about survival have been settled through our willingness to die to this weak, frightened, ineffective life. Fasting has removed the sting of death and sealed our resolve once and for all.

Now we are ready for the resurrection life that can only take place from a soul that has been put to death in order to be transformed. The very essence of our new life in Christ is His resurrected body, and how this power of resurrection comes to substitute the old sinful nature. Resurrection is not the ultimate goal of a Christian life, but its very beginning, the source from which everything else springs forth.

> Therefore we are buried with him by baptism into death; that like as Christ was raised up from the dead by the glory of the Father, even so we also should walk in newness of life. For if we have been planted together in the likeness of his death, we shall be also in the likeness of his resurrection.
>
> —*Romans 6:4-5*

Because we have His resurrection in us (If indeed we have died to sin) the spirit realm opens up before us with new thoughts and images. Our hearts are free to love and experience what Ephesians 3:18-19 says,

To know the love of Christ this passes knowledge;
that you may be filled with all the fullness of God.

That verse will have meaning now because you have
a heart and a mind that can receive from the Father. We
have moved into a relationship that we have read about
but not understood because of our former condition.

The soul is no longer fragmented, double-minded, or
with rollercoaster feelings, but we are whole and capable
of loving God with all our heart, mind and soul.

The passion is back and we are burning for the One
who has captivated our heart from the beginning. The life
we have been living till now makes no sense without Jesus
ruling it from the inside out. We have found the purpose
for which we were created and we are in love and capable
of expressing true love.

That love has a name and it is Jesus, the lover of our
souls. That love has healed our broken heart and poured
the oil of the Holy Ghost over our fragmented soul.

In this condition we are now able to look at Scriptures
in the Bible and see the Spirit of God. The designs of God
make sense and we start to understand a higher calling.
His purposes for our life begin to unfold in such a way as
to prepare us for a place of kingdom authority.

**The reforming of our souls is just the beginning.
The journey God has for all of us will take many
more years than our earthly bodies will allow. I
believe that is why God put the tree of life in the**

garden. His plans are so beyond our natural life that they will take hundreds of years to fulfill.

The doors we have opened by the keys to the designs of God are revealing rooms of enormous wealth and power. These are not the wealth of this world but the wealth of the riches of His glory.

The power is not measurable by the standards of this world but through the authority God gives to command circumstances and demons. Now we begin to see why our association with the things of this world system must not hold any attraction or desire. This is why we have experienced and will continue to experience more testing to ensure our heart's reformation process is preceding thoroughly.

The next chapter follows the sequence of revelations Jesus unfolded in Matthew 6. Our condition spiritually will depend on the levels of our obedience thus far. Jesus has prepared and trained us for dominating the enemy by the way He lived on this planet.

The revelations through His words and actions are designed for us to dominate from kingdom authority. There is a battle in which every Church, unknowingly for most, is participating.

We spoke about this false god previously but we will now study the spirit of Mammon in greater detail. The preparation we have had until now is for this encounter. So with the level of our current understanding and the release of the wisdom from the Holy Spirit, we will expose this anti-Christ.

The roots of this spirit are deep inside each of us, and very subtle. We are all subject to this devil and have tasted of the wine of her fornication to the point of intoxication.

The detoxification process will require the keys the Holy Spirit has given us. They will unlock the doors that will release the weapons designed for our deliverance.

This will begin another exodus not unlike what we have read concerning the first one from Egypt. I believe the cries of God's people have reached His ears once again because of the bondage of His people. We are slaves of the worst kind because we believe we are free. But we are about to discover the captor and what it will take for freedom.

4

The Master's Key

Before we can understand the purpose of this chapter we need to make sure we have used the keys the Holy Spirit has provided. All of the keys to this point, in our discussion, are to expose our soul's condition. We have been conditioned to believe certain things that may or may not be true. When I say conditioned I mean that what we hear over and over we will believe. This type of structure is how most of us are trained to make our life's choices. These choices are made regardless of whether what we hear is the truth or not.

Therefore, the truth is what must be used to identify our false beliefs. Jesus said:

> If you remain in my words you will become my disciples and KNOW the truth which will set you free.
>
> —*John 8:31-32*

Jesus is the truth and the life as spoken in John 14:6, which means life is not lived in truth, without the One who is truth living through us.

Using the above Scriptures as our foundation for determining the truth we are now capable of making sound decisions on what we should believe based on the word of God. Then step by step we use the keys of giving, praying, and fasting, to open up the regions of our heart and mind.

We must be cognizant of the fact that we are uncovering years and years of wrong thinking which has created layers upon layers of wrong believing. Now, with the help of the Holy Spirit, we can continue the journey of uprooting the wrong thinking from within our hearts and move from "glory to glory".

These false structures reside within our souls. They are hidden in the thoughts of our mind, heart and emotions. These beliefs are idols or "false gods" which are easily identified as thoughts that represent our reliance and are the focus of our attention. These "gods" are the essence of our security and trust. These "gods" come in the form of money, power, and position. The "trappings" or observable features of these gods can be found in cars, houses, material pleasures, extravagant entertainments or escapes. We are all prisoners and slaves of our false trusts and securities.

The keys we have received are given to reveal the levels of captivity within our souls. Each key is designed to open our own personal doors, where we are controlled by wrong belief strongholds of the mind and heart. As we discover these impediments our weapons of giving, praying and fasting begin to uproot and pull down these inner structures.

These doors are compartments within our souls that contain a systematic design to make bad decisions from regions of darkness. I say systematic because the enemy has trained us through many fear tactics. For example, I recall making my choices in school according to how much money I could make concerning a career after graduation. I was primarily motivated by the fear of not being able to provide myself with a sufficient income. This is unfortunately the motivation of many Christians today. The motivation is not to please the Father but to satisfy the fear of not having enough money. This is the systematic approach I am speaking about to pervert the Truth of Jesus with the lies of this world's system.

When we are made aware of this wrong thinking and believing, we become determined to free ourselves from these prisons. However, If we use the kingdom of this world as a bell weather for discerning right from wrong, we will create more darkness within our minds. The Apostle James wrote:

> Do you not know that to be a lover of the world means enmity with God? Therefore, whoever wants to be a lover of the world makes himself an enemy of God.
>
> — *James 4:4*

The darkness is the result of not having the light of the glorious gospel, and this applies to unbelievers and to Christians who are full of unbelief.

> In which the prince of this world hath blinded the minds of them which believe not, lest the light of the glorious gospel of Christ who is the image of God, should sine unto them.
>
> —*2 Corinthians 4:4*

Our souls are made up of the mind, heart, emotions, and will. This design makes our souls very complex and the place where the battle lines are drawn between man, Satan and God. This is the region in man that has been dominated by Satan beginning at our birth. It is also where we must exercise our choice of what voices we will choose to believe. If we heed any voice other than the Spirit of God our soul will be fragmented and chaotic. It is this fragmentation that requires major surgery by the Holy Spirit. This spiritual surgery is accomplished by many ways. One of the ways this can be accomplished is through the designs we are discovering in this book.

The "Lover of our souls" has given us keys to take us step by step, battle by battle, to defeat the destroyer of our souls. Each key is designed to open the doors of our captured mind, heart and emotions and release us into the fullness of knowing our precious Savior. Man is so "bound up" and captive by generations upon generations of iniquity and sin that his soul, with all its complexities, has been tremendously damaged. This requires a loving

Father to "undo" the harm. This process can be painful and frightening if we do not depend solely upon the Holy Spirit for direction.

This is the dilemma in all of us. We have been taught that once we recite the "sinner's prayer" that something dramatically changes within our souls which allows us to be controlled by the Spirit.

Most Christian Churches focus on the Scripture in Roman 10:9-10 as the basis for receiving the lost into the kingdom of God. However, if we observe the key wording of this verse we will discover something that has caused the Church such consternation with its new converts. The words, "believe in thine heart....with the heart man believeth unto righteousness; and with the mouth confession is made unto salvation."

The condition of our heart is such, that believing something as life changing as the gospel will not go uncontested by the one who has dominated our heart, which is Satan. The truth is most of us begin our journey in similar conditions but if the seed of salvation is really to take root and grow our life can never be the same as it was when we first made that confession. The simple word repentance, often omitted in the "sinners prayer", separate the ones who die to this life and begin their journey as "new creatures". (2 Corinthians 5:17)

The soul is where our struggles begin and end. The purpose of our life is not necessarily survival.

Let me explain that statement. If I come to the cross of Christ with preconceived ideas on how to be a "disciple" then I have not left everything to follow Him. If I do not come to the cross with the complete persuasion that my life does not belong to me any longer then, as the scriptures says I cannot call myself His disciple. (Luke 14:26)

The purpose of our life is exactly what Jesus said His life's purpose was in John 10:17, when He said;

I gladly lay down my life that I may pick it up again.

The principal of loosing your life that you may find it again is also dramatically presented in Matthew 10:38,

And he that taketh, not his cross and followed after me, is not worthy of me.

Jesus knew the purpose of His life, He could not be corrupted in His soul, by self promotion and survival motivations.

The soul of man is where the enemy focuses to destroy our relationship with the Father; it began in the Garden of Eden.

This focus has not changed today. When Jesus went to the Garden of Gethsemane, He did many things:

One, He showed Satan that this garden was going to be the place of obedience, not disobedience. Two, Jesus was making a way so every man's soul could enter through their own gardens to the cross and then to freedom.

The garden of Gethsemane for all of us must be the night we wrestle with our souls to give up this world and all of its attachments. That method is still the only way and the only door for all ages to come. No power in Hell can hold the soul of man who is willing to lay down his life for the sake of the only true Lord and Master.

When we truly understand the weakness in our souls, we begin the process designed by the Holy Spirit to bring us back to the Father.

Our weaknesses are known by the enemy because Lucifer lost his position in heaven for the same reasons man lost his. I am speaking of our souls being impregnated with the same iniquity found in Satan. This iniquity produces souls whose thoughts are conceived for only one purpose, self exaltation and survival.

The wisdom of God is so transforming that when we are introduced to this knowledge through the Holy Spirit, our mind, heart and emotions can be renewed. This can only happen when we are unencumbered by our soul's insatiable desire for control and survival.

The wisdom of God is inconceivable by a soul with generations of iniquity and sin. The Master knew this about our condition and developed strategies to bring us out of captivity.

The keys we are receiving are designed to release us from each level of our soul's imprisonment. The key of giving takes us from the grip of our thoughts of fear of loss. The key of prayer unlocks the gates of our hearts to receive directly from the Holy Spirit. The key of fasting is the weapon that controls the body and destroys the soul's desire for self survival at "all costs."

In this chapter something dramatic is going to happen. Up to this point the precious Holy Spirit has been giving us keys to unlock the doors of our soul. But now we are going to become the "Master's Key" against the number one enemy of our soul, THE SPIRIT OF MAMMON.

We are going to be the key in the hand of the Holy Spirit to lock the doors of our soul from serving false gods. No more will the enemy consume our thoughts, bind our emotions and create in us a divided heart. We have already seen that God demands us to follow Him with an undivided heart, but He also enable us to do it.

> Teach me your way, O Lord, that I may walk in your truth; give me an undivided heart to revere your name.
>
> —*Psalm 86:11*

Becoming the Master's Key is worthy of research and understanding. Let me share with you what I have received from the Holy Spirit.

Years ago I realized how easy it was for me to be held captive by my emotions. I would begin many days filled with hope and faith that I could maintain my focus continually on the Lord.

I would have awakened early in the morning to spend time in prayer and worship, and encountered an awesome presence of God. Then would come a phone call that immediately interrupted the presence of God with the sound of anger and hostility from someone.

My goal of continually thinking about the Lord was broken and my emotions were filled with grief and anxiety.

The roller coaster ride of our emotions takes us from the heights of bliss to the depths of despair in a matter of seconds. Maybe this has happened to you.

As I enquired about this turmoil in my soul, the precious Holy Spirit began to reveal some truths to me that I believe can help us overcome this situation in our lives.

The components of our souls are so intricately woven together between our thoughts, heart and emotions that when we affect one part we touch all.

For example, when my emotions were afflicted by someone's anger, my mind triggered an emotion in the form of an image to send to my heart. These images were comprised of sensations which shaped or formed the way I perceived the person or event.

In other words, when I left the presence of God (the only true Judge) and entered into my non-transformed soul to process what my senses were receiving all kinds of ungodly thoughts were released.

These images contained some truths and information about what I was receiving. But by no means was I receiving the complete truth. I was making evaluations and judgments from a soul filled with corrupted images.

We are all trained to trust what we are feeling as the truth in order to protect our own image. This is the essence of our problem.

The purpose of becoming the "master's key" is so that we are no longer attached to our images. These images of ourselves that we protect, promote and cultivate are no longer important or real. The only image we must have is that of Christ.

Nothing says it so clearly as Paul in Colossians 3:1-11,

So if you have been raised with Christ, seek the things that are above, where Christ is, seated at the right hand of God. Set your minds on things that are above, not on things that are on earth, for you have died, and your life is hidden with Christ in God. When Christ who is your life is revealed, then you also will be revealed with him in glory.

Put to death, therefore, whatever in you is earthly: fornication, impurity, passion, evil desire, and greed (which is idolatry). On account of these the wrath of God is coming on those who are disobedient. These are the ways you also once followed, when you were living that life. But now you must get rid of all such things—anger, wrath, malice, slander, and abusive language from your mouth. Do not lie to one another, seeing that you have stripped off the old self with its practices and have clothed yourselves with the new self, which is being renewed in knowledge according to the image of its creator. In that renewal there is no longer Greek and Jew, circumcised and uncircumcised, barbarian, Scythian, slave and free; but Christ is all and in all!

The master's key shuts the door of wrong images and opens the door to THE TRUE IMAGE. The image we who are bought with the price of His blood must bear. Jesus, who bore the image of His father, requires us to bear His image.

Remember in Revelation 3:7 we see that Jesus who has the Key of David is the only one who can shut what no man can open and open what no man can shut. David became the master's key and it is this key we are speaking about. I believe every generation must walk in the authority of David on this earth. Time or space does not permit me to elaborate on the life of David. Suffice it to say that David is the symbol of Messianic Authority and true prosperity for the end time. If you study the origin of the "key of David," you will see it originates in Isaiah 22:22 when Elikiam was promoted as treasurer and prime minister to protect the plans of God during the eventual captivity into Babylon.

If we become the "master's key," even if we are in captivity in Babylon, we will be used to extricate ourselves and those with whom we have been entrusted into the kingdom of God. All I can say is 'Halleluiah!'"

Now let us return to Matthew 6 and begin again with verse 19. We are going to understand this revelation from the perspective of the Father who wants us free from the bondage of our unrenewed souls.

Do not lay up for yourselves treasures on earth, where moth and rust destroy and where thieves break in and steal; but lay up for yourselves treasures in heaven, where neither moth nor rust destroys and where thieves do not break in and steal. For where your treasure is, there your heart will be also.

The word used here to represent treasures takes on a different meaning when our riches are now in the form of Jesus. Now our thinking is being transformed and our values are under major reconstruction.

When Jesus was confronting the young rich man, He said something that can give us light on Matthew 19:20-22.

If you want to be perfect, go, sell what you have and give to the poor and you will have treasure in heaven; and come, follow me.
But when the young man heard that saying, he went away sorrowful: for he had great possessions.

Here, the principles we have been establishing are plainly shown to this rich man. Jesus is saying, in essence: if you want real wealth, give away what you have and follow Me. Or, be willing to die to everything you think is valuable and "life supporting" and follow My kingdom directives.

The treasure Jesus is talking about is "the pearl of great price" spoken of in the gospels. This understanding is so beyond our way of evaluating the true wealth that Jesus has to make a strong illustration to his disciples. He goes on, saying:

> ...Verily I say unto you, it is easier for a camel to go through the eye of a needle, than for a rich man to enter into the kingdom of God.
>
> When his disciples heard it, they were exceedingly amazed, saying, "Who then can be saved?"
>
> But Jesus beheld them, and said unto them, "With men this is impossible; but for God all things are possible."
>
> —*Mathew 19:23-26*

Jesus tells His disciples how hard it is for the rich to be saved. It is obvious from the response of the disciples that they also thought righteousness and riches were synonyms.

But the interesting point Jesus is making is that with God the spirit of this world can be broken. Notice, He says, "with God all things are possible." Our trust in God is shallow for many reasons, but mainly because Mammon has perverted what is truly valuable. Jesus also stated,

> what is considered valuable with man is an abomination with God.
>
> —*Luke 16:15*

The essence of what Jesus is teaching cannot be understood without searching deep within our souls. Our souls can be dissected to discover the makeup of the heart, mind and emotions. If we can find where our ideas and convictions are formed, then perhaps we can witness a transformation within our very beings.

Transforming Our Thought Life: The Human Soul

We are going to enter into more detail about thoughts and the effect they have on our soul. The purpose of this is to make us aware of how our souls operate. The human soul is mainly composed of three elements, which are, the heart, mind and emotions.

Jesus made a statement in Mark 12:29-30 that will help clarify the purpose of our study about the soul. He said, "The Lord our God is ONE Lord: And we are to love Him with all our heart, all our soul, and with our entire mind and all our strength."

The Scripture in Genesis 1:26-27 says, "Let us make man in our image after our likeness." We know from our previous discussion that man lost that image as a result of his disobedience. This has resulted in the present condition of our souls being fragmented and divided. I believe our soul at creation was complete, heart, mind and emotions. But this is not the condition now and Jesus knew this and was in essence saying in Mark, if we are to be one the way He, the Father and Holy Spirit are one, then it must be in our spirit, soul and body.

How many times I have known in my heart that I should read my Bible and pray but was negotiated from that position by my minds fatigue or fear. Or how many times have I made a schedule to engage in early morning worship and devotions to be denied by a body whose desires were to stay in bed and sleep.

That is why I am convinced that Matthew 6 is one of the designs the Holy Spirit is using to reconstruct our souls into the image from which they were created.

1) The MIND is much more than just the brain of man. The brain is a major component of the mind, but to say the brain is the mind would be like saying the roar of the lion is the lion.

We can observe many of the results of our machine called the brain but we can not see our mind. The brain is capable of the following functions reason, learning, and memory. We have the ability to invent, create, store information and understand concepts. We can also daydream, imagine things as well as process, and receive information. An analogy that can be helpful to visualize the brain would be to imagine the most sophisticated of computers. Scientists tell us that man uses only a small percentage of its capacities. It is easy to understand why Western cultures believe within the brain of man lie all the wisdom necessary for immortality. We can observe many of the miraculous functions of the brain but the Bible speaks about the need to transform our minds. Therefore, I think it is relvant to understand the mind as in relation to the Scriptures.

So where does this leave the philosophers, the scholars, and the world's brilliant debaters? God has made them all look foolish and has shown their wisdom to be useless nonsense. Since God in his wisdom saw to it that the world would never find him through human wisdom, he has used our foolish preaching to save all who believe. God's way seems foolish to the Jews because they want a sign from heaven to prove it is true. And it is foolish to the Greeks because they believe only what agrees with their own wisdom. So when we preach that Christ was crucified, the Jews are offended, and the Gentiles say it's all nonsense. But to those called by God to salvation, both Jews and Gentiles, Christ is the mighty power of God and the wonderful wisdom of God. This "foolish" plan of God is far wiser than the wisest of human plans, and God's weakness is far stronger than the greatest of human strength.

—*1 Corinthians 1:20-25*

Yet when I am among mature Christians, I do speak with words of wisdom, but not the kind of wisdom that belongs to this world, and not the kind that appeals to the rulers of this world, who are being brought to nothing. No, the wisdom we speak of is the secret wisdom of God, which was hidden in former times, though he made it for our benefit before the world began. But the rulers of this world have not understood it; if they had, they would never have crucified our glorious Lord. That is what the Scriptures mean when they say,

No eye has seen, no ear has heard,

and no mind has imagined
what God has prepared
for those who love him.

But we know these things because God has revealed
them to us by his Spirit, and his Spirit searches out
everything and shows us even God's deep secrets.
No one can know what anyone else is really thinking
except that person alone, and no one can know
God's thoughts except God's own Spirit. And God
has actually given us his Spirit (not the world's
spirit) so we can know the wonderful things God
has freely given us. When we tell you this, we do
not use words of human wisdom. We speak words
given to us by the Spirit, using the Spirit's words to
explain spiritual truths. But people who aren't Christians can't understand these truths from God's Spirit.
It all sounds foolish to them because only those who
have the Spirit can understand what the Spirit means.
We who have the Spirit understand these things, but
others can't understand us at all. How could they?
For,

Who can know what the Lord is thinking?
Who can give him counsel?

But we can understand these things, for we have the
mind of Christ.

—1 Corinthians 2:1-16

Paul is saying that the spirit of man and the Spirit of God are capable of communing together through wisdom, but not the wisdom of this world. **The wisdom of this world is confined to problem solving from a limited understanding of man's origin and purpose.** Therefore, the mind of man, which is located in our soul must be transformed or renewed as Romans 12:2 says.

2) The emotions are our responses to stimuli from within us and from the outside. It is one way we are conditioned to respond to events and circumstances surrounding our environments. I say conditioned, because we attempt to avoid pain and gravitate toward pleasure. Emotions are the most basic of avenues available to the enemy to control man. Emotions are the primary link between our physical senses and the soul. Emotions are very important in the make-up of man's soul and must be trained to engage the Spirit of God for instructions in maturing this part of our soul..

3) The heart is not only the pump in our chest cavity. It is also the center where all thoughts and emotions are processed. The heart is the engine or the driving force of the soul. The heart is to the spirit of man what emotions are to the body or carnal part of our three part being.

The heart is the place where the energy of the thoughts and emotions is transformed into pictures or images. It is the center from which the soul gets its direction, prejudices, and belief systems. The heart, soul and spirit are sometimes interchanged in the Bible (Ezekiel. 36:26), and is strictly a translator's interpretation.

The heart has the capacity to believe anything in the Bible as long as it remains innocent and pure. The fall of Adam transformed the fleshy or innocent heart into one of stone. (Ezekiel. 36:25-27).

This is why Jesus kept comparing little children to the way to enter into the kingdom- because they believe with an innocent and pure heart.

So it is obvious to me that this is where believing originates and is where faith is realized.

In order to become the Master's key, in the hands of the Lord the soul needs to be totally transformed into light.

In order for this to happen let me share some revelations that the Holy Spirit has shown me.

Through the following Scripture, we are going to grasp something extraordinary related to our "thought life." This will help us to understand the physical and spiritual make-up of our thoughts.

> The lamp of the body is the eye. If therefore your eye is good, your whole body will be full of light. But if your eye is bad, your whole body will be full of darkness. If therefore the light that is in you is darkness, how great is that darkness!
>
> —*Mathew 6:22-23*

If we exchange the word "soul" for the word "eye", and the word "thoughts" for the word "lamp", then we'll be able to see something revelatory for our lives, and that is the tremendous importance our thought life has in the process of our becoming light.

Thoughts And Why They Are Important

Let us examine something that will help us understand our purpose in this part of the discussion. In Romans 7:15-25 Paul is expressing his absolute frustration with what he knew he should do but was unable to do because of the law of sin in his mind and body. Where did that law originate and how did he overcome this condition?

The law of sin and death are a result of mans disobedience, beginning in Genesis till now, our minds and bodies have been sold into the slavery of sin and dominated by the will of Satan. What's more, we have been recreated in his image, not God's, with his mind and his future. The Father, knowing our predicament made arrangements for our return to His image by the radical transformation, beginning at the cross of Jesus with our death and then the reformation of our mind and body by changing what, who and how we think.

This transformation process is one of the most important parts of our study in Matthew 6. Paul tells us what to think about in Philippians 4:8-9. He tells us how to do it in 2 Corinthians 10:3. Then Jesus releases the Holy Spirit as the who that will perform the perfecting of our souls in John 14:23-28.

Becoming the Master's Key is impossible if we do not become the "mind of Christ" as stated in 1 Corinthians 2:15. Paul knew that walking in the Spirit was the only way one could have the mind of Christ.

When we understand that our thoughts are what the enemy of our soul seeks to dominate by fear and doubt and our only weapon against that domination is the Word of God and the Holy Ghost. Then we will become very vigilant in our efforts to guard our minds and "host" the Holy Ghost with the reverence He deserves.

The purpose of my trying to explain the thought realm is to help us move beyond our minds into the spirit realm. The secret of Matthew 6:22-23 is contained in our ability to understand how to control our thought life. Our thoughts will take on a totally different understanding if we can see that they must become His thoughts if we are ever to reach our destiny in Him.

What Creates In Us The Desire To Think Or Behave One Way Or The Other?

Motivation

This question can best be understood by analyzing our lives.

In observing my own life I find that what continually motivates me to think or act one way or another depends on the positive or negative reinforcement I receive.

For example, if I am continually condemned and rebuked for not cleaning my room, I may not be inclined to clean it up at all.

The opposite of this example is that if I am continually rewarded by appropriate complements, I am more likely to continue cleaning my room.

What We Continually Hear

The amazing thing about our soul's composition is that what we hear long enough we will believe. That is why the scripture says,

> So then faith comes by hearing, (and hearing and hearing) the word of God.
>
> —*Romans 10:17*

The soul is the soil and the seeds are what we continually hear. If we listen to doubt and unbelief we will produce fruit inside of our souls that are full of poisons, darkness and death. The heart which is our believing center will be corrupted and unable to believe the word of God.

Therefore, our responsibility is to convert our souls to the image of God found within our spirit. The Bible speaks about having the "mind of Christ" (2 Corinthians 2:10). The reborn spirit of man must be in control of his soul, or his life will be a series of constant battles and conflicts. This is an all too familiar situation in our Churches today.

What We Continually Think

Our lives are controlled by what we think about. We will move our lives in the direction in which we continually think. Saying it in another way, if one continually thinks about becoming a millionaire, one will find himself consumed with those types of mental pictures.

For example, one might surround oneself with images or conversations of expensive cars, expensive clothes, big houses and expensive restaurants. The conversations of this person will nearly always have the words, "costs", "money", "worth", "how much", " can or cannot afford it" etcetera.

The same is true for negative thoughts, such as in an illness. A sick person may surround herself with all kinds' of images of sickness and disease. She may read much information about medicines, or the latest medical discoveries. She may listen very attentively to any person speaking about symptoms, or diseases and death.

The distinction between images and pictures is important. The heart of man stores images in order to form beliefs and feel secure. **The mind paints pictures because it has been trained to function more quickly and efficiently than the other parts of our soul.** The mind must make fast decisions based on less information than the heart or emotional centers of the soul. This is why pictures may not be complete but like pencil sketches on an artists easel.

Images And Pictures

Thoughts and words begin to form pictures in our minds and eventually images in our heart.

For example, if someone talks about a disease or sickness, we are capable of retrieving an image of the last time we had the symptoms or malady.

Pictures are the quickest way for our minds to associate with what we like and what we dislike. Images we like are usually associated with things that give us security, pleasure, happiness, etc. The opposite is true for images that we do not like which are associated with anxiety, fear, doubt and turmoil. They form structures that can be strongholds of captivity.

Images, whether right or wrong, enrich, or corrupt our hearts. Images from the word of God and people of faith strengthen our relationship with the Spirit of God.

One of the major purposes of God's Word is to feed our spirits with the image of God. That image will overpower all the images of fear and doubt.

The Spirit of God reforms the image we lost in the Garden, through Adam's disobedience. In addition, our spirit starts to control what we think about, and who we listen to, both spiritually and physically.

The Belief System

Many times what we believe has little to do with the truth. What is relative truth for each of us is determined by the information we decide is valuable or trust worthy.

This is one of the processes by which our lives are guided. We have always been given the choice to trust God and His ways, or to make our own decisions in this life regardless of the Bible.

Romans 10:9-10 says ("with the HEART man believes for righteousness . . . ") Then he confesses with his mouth. Our hearts must be convinced before our mouths will change their words.

Perhaps many who have been unsuccessful at confessing the word of God needed to check their heart condition.

I am not necessarily saying that such people are not saved (even though some may not be) but that their motives may be wrong. The heart is directly affected by what it believes.

Our "thought life" paints the pictures and our hearts are the canvas that displays these impressions. These imprints become images and these images become belief systems.

Our heart's belief system determines our behavior. The heart believes and behaves according to what it is continually forced to hear, see and meditate on.

The mind will believe most things that give it pleasure, profit and security. The heart on the other hand will make it's decision to believe according to the images that it has formed from the pictures it has received.

When the heart believes something different from that of the mind the soul begins to become fragmented and chaotic.

For example, if I am trained in my mind to believe only what I can see, feel, touch and taste, and the Bible and my heart say, faith is believing what you can not see and that is what pleases God, I have a dilemma and a major chaos rages within my soul. .

The Apostle Paul understood very well the importance of our thought life. He instructed us on what we should think about,

Finally, beloved, whatever is true, whatever is honorable, whatever is just, whatever is pure, whatever is pleasing, whatever is commendable, if there is any

excellence and if there is anything worthy of praise, think about these things. Keep on doing the things that you have learned and received and heard and seen in me, and the God of peace will be with you
—*Philippians 4:8-9*

We must see the importance of our thoughts in relation to our heart and how this ultimately affects the completeness of our soul.

The Bible continually says we must seek God with our whole heart, mind and soul. (Mark 12:30-31) How is this possible when our heart believes one thing and our mind another?

As a child I noticed something strategically designed by the enemy to corrupt the beliefs of our hearts.

Like most children I grew up with the so called "harmless belief" in Santa Clause. I was continually told the "lie" about this fat man, who wore a beard and flew a sleigh pulled by reindeer. This fictional character delivered gifts every Christmas, to "good" children, by sliding down the fireplace chimney.

That time of year, which was originally intended to celebrate the birth of Jesus, became a time of celebrating this make believe man, that brought all of our "goodies".

Then as I matured, my mentality was turned to skepticism for having believed this lie. The sinister plan of the enemy had succeeded. My heart filled with possibility to believe was changed to doubt and mistrust.

So why would I believe there was a Jesus born to a virgin? The same thing happened at Easter with the Easter Bunny.

Our belief systems formed within our hearts become so by the information we process, that we make into images. These images have nothing to do with the truth, unless they are founded on Gods word and His image.

Restoring Our Souls

The image of God in man was lost in the fall of Adam and restored through the resurrection of Jesus.

> Now the Lord is the Spirit, and where the Spirit of the Lord is, there is freedom. And all of us, with unveiled faces, seeing the glory of the Lord as though reflected in a mirror, are being transformed into the same image from one degree of glory to another; for this comes from the Lord, the Spirit.
>
> —*2 Corinthians 3:17-18*

Being conformed to the image of God is a progressive transformation that requires the reformation of the soul. This is a project for the ages and must begin while we are in this body and on this planet.

As we have learned through this chapter, the thoughts of man are important to God. We have seen how the thoughts of God are the only tool capable of conforming us into the True Light.

The thoughts of God are higher than our thoughts and indeed are more powerful than the weapons of this age.

The purpose of this book has been designed to impart keys for unlocking our souls and setting us free. God is challenging us to believe the way Jesus believed.

If we can do nothing else, we must go to Philippians 4:8 and start thinking on the things Paul speaks about.

We have come too far to go back. The life we are now living is going to change into a life that reflects the image of God.

This will require for each of us to continually check what we believe against what God says. Not what some one said, that you thought you heard. But you must study the Bible for yourself.

The Word + Giving + Prayer + Fasting = God's Image.

God's image is what we are after and what I am going to obtain.

How about you?

5
Mammon

We have now reached the "WHY" for becoming the Master's Key. All of the keys of giving, praying and fasting have prepared us for this end time battle. The power of our adversary and the reasons for our slavery will be made clear. Our enemy is Mammon and our souls have been his resting place.

As we discovered in the previous chapter, we become the key the Master uses to open doors no man can shut and close doors no man can open. That key is the ultimate weapon used by Jesus, formed from the lives of those who have used "the keys."

I trust you have noticed by now, the kingdom of God operates by rewarding those who have mastered the keys of giving, praying and fasting, with more authority and challenges. The biggest one we will all face is defeating the spirit of Mammon in our lives. Let's follow along in Matthew:

No one can serve two masters; for either he will hate the one and love the other, or else he will be loyal to the one and despise the other. You cannot serve God and Mammon.

—*Matthew 6: 24*

Why would Jesus put this verse in this place? We have said all along, that God is a God of design, purpose and timing. Jesus knew there was no reason to speak about Mammon until we were equipped to defeat it.

But He also knows the composition of the human being, particularly the complexity of the soul. He knows unless our soul and flesh are one with His Spirit, we are helpless to change masters, or even recognize the difference.

What is the most important commandment?
Jesus answered, The most important one says: "People of Israel, you have only one Lord and God. You must love him with all your heart, soul, mind, and strength."

—*Mark 12:28-30*

This statement is the heart of what we have been discussing throughout our book.

How can we love the Lord our God with all of our being? How do we fix our soul and body (strength) to be one with Him the way Jesus was one with His Father?

We have said all along that Jesus in His infinite love and wisdom developed the teachings found in Matthew 6 for this very reason. This is why we are developing our lives of giving, praying and fasting, to repair our souls.

We have used each key to open chambers within our minds and hearts to let the "light of the Holy Spirit" shine inside. This light allows us to replace our fears with faith and see the end from the beginning.

"So what exactly is Mammon?" you might say. Some translations use the word "money" in place of Mammon. This is not an accurate translation but someone's interpretation. Money has its own Greek word and is used throughout the Scriptures. Mammon is an Aramaic word which means, "That which is kept safe, or secured." Thus, because so many believe security is in money, then it is easy to see how the translators have interposed money for the true name of this spirit.

However, Mammon is a spirit that manifests in property, stocks, careers, or family connections or anything which subtly guarantees and secures an income. In ancient Israel, this spirit was the direct equivalent to what we now call "savings." A man's mammon was his bank account, his safety net against the unforeseen. When a Jew of ancient Palestine referred to his Mammon, he was speaking of that thing that GUARANTEED his financial security. MAMMON IS ANYTHING WE PUT OUR TRUST IN OTHER THAN GOD. ANYTHING!!!!!!!!!!!!!!!!!!!!!!!!!!!!!!

Mammon is not necessarily money, but that which gives the power to purchase what money can buy. It is a type of promissory note that gives an illusion to it's owners of security and purchasing power. I say illusion because if anyone who has read about or lived during the great depression in the United States can see how one day money had worth and the next day it did not. This is one high price for serving Mammon.

Mammon Perverts The Message Of Prosperity

So when Jesus compares God and Mammon, He is referring to the system, which is a spirit, that competes for the affection, worship, faith and attention of those who say, "Lord, Lord."

All my Christian life I thought I was serving God. I was a giver in tithes and offerings over and above 50% of my income. At that time in my life I was making several thousand dollars a month. I secretly began to admire my giving to the point that pride and arrogance became associated with my giving.

I would choose carefully those ministers and ministries to whom I would give or "sow" into. The primary purpose that I gave to them was number one; I was being nurtured and fed in my spiritual development.

These Men of God were very popular in the media and throughout the world. I felt good about giving to ministries that I could watch on TV and see how millions of lives were being affected. The other reason was, I believed that God would multiply back what I gave. All of these ministers taught sowing and reaping. Sometimes that is all they taught. But there were other benefits to giving into those ministries as well. I would be recognized for the amount of my giving by special seating at conferences, or I would be given so-called private numbers directly to the ministers' homes.

The larger the gift the more the recognition and special privileges. Some ministries would invite me to become part of their "inner circle" of followers, which allowed me access to selected meetings and trips with them personally.

I felt very privileged to have personal contacts with some of the biggest personalities in the Christian and Television world. Each of these men was serious about their passion for Jesus and the hurting millions in the world.

But, the system being used to keep their ministries going was creating something other than what was intended. I observed that the people operating these ministries were using the same techniques and principles as common corporations of the world used.

I watched as the same "Madison Avenue" slick advertisement to sell cars, or elect politicians, was employed to promote the conferences and persuade me to give to these ministries.

I received multiplied thousands of dollars in publicity and newsletters a year from many ministries that I was supporting. The bigger ones were like a corporation, who had to have more and more money to operate their many departments and expenses.

The men of God became more like CEO's of huge enterprises, than what I had imagined an evangelist, healer or teacher of the gospel should be. I am not intending to judge anyone here. I am relating my feelings, and what God was teaching me about my heart and about the system of Mammon.

I began to feel like giving entitled me to get from God. In fact I was starting to get subliminal messages from these ministries that having money was a sign of righteousness.

I began to feel that because I was not receiving "the hundred-fold return," there must have been something wrong in my spiritual life. I believed that those who had lots of money had great faith. After all, some ministries talked extensively about how many planes they owned and had given away in their lives.

I never met one person who received a hundred-fold from their giving. There might be many. I just have not heard or read of any.

But in the circles that I frequented that message, which has since been replaced with the "thousand fold," was the most popular teaching presented before an offering was taken.

There was not one person among us who did not think after giving in that offering, that we would be entitled to receive what would be equivalent to the lottery. That is how corrupted my heart had become from thinking about being prosperous.

Let me make this clear, I believe each of those men to be absolutely convinced God was being honored in their lives and ministries. Indeed, all of these men are precious saints of God full of integrity and I am not their judge.

Moreover, I would not even have reached the first step of giving had it not been for the messages from these men of God.

We are living in a new generation that must hear and see much more the nature and true character of God.

I am convinced that God initiated the so-called "prosperity" message for a major reason. That reason is because the Church did and in many places still does not, give.

The Church is still so bound up in Mammon that many of its members do not even tithe. So God had to show the Church through His mercy that He is a rewarder of those who will diligent seek Him, even if it is in the most elementary ways, such as giving.

I began to notice over a period of several months that my business was "drying up." The business that I believed God had blessed as a result of my giving to His work was becoming like the "brook of Cherith" in 1 Kings 17:7.

Then one day my money ran out. I had not done anything differently. I was giving all that I had to the ministries who were regularly asking, sometimes two and three times a month.

But my business was not producing any income. I was self-employed and relied on what I thought was God to prosper me. "What is wrong? Lord, I asked. I heard nothing from the Holy Spirit.

During those years of giving tens of thousands of dollars, I had gone to many nations. I had prayed for the sick and had seen miracles. I prophesied and cast out devils and even preached. I was truly being used by God and felt His presence often. So why was I not receiving the hundred-fold returns as promised? Why had my prayers for money gone unanswered?

Then the Holy Spirit said,: "Read the following scriptures: Matthew 7:20-24" This speaks about those who had cast out devils, prophesied and done miracles in His name. But He told them, "DEPART FROM ME, I NEVER KNEW YOU, FOR YOUR PRACTICE IS EVIL IN MY EYES."

Then the Holy Spirit said clearly, "your master is Mammon not me." I was absolutely devastated. How could this be? I knew I had heard the Holy Spirit tell me to give to these ministries. I knew that my "sowing" entitled me to "reaping" according to the Bible. I knew all of these truths.

However, more times than not the hidden motivation is for our "financial security." This is where our deception begins and the transfer of allegiance from one master to another takes place

But my giving was to a disguised system from a wrong heart, based upon the principles of Mammon. My trust was not in God but in the system of "giving and getting."

I had heard these mighty men of God say over and over, while they were taking an offering "your source is God, not your job."

That was "a truth" alright but I for one did not know the difference. I was also taught that God could use my job to prosper me. So, subtly the job and God was confused in my mind on who was really supplying.

I had listened to the biblical principles on how to prosper perverted by the system of Mammon. What truly began as a revelation from God, corrupted my way of thinking by appealing to my sin nature of greed that had not been transformed.

We were told by some to have multiple streams of money; to create a hedge against financial disaster. Some were even teaching us to have faith in faith, but not how to have faith in God. I was seeking to live well but I was drinking at the Well of Mammon.

Let me repeat, I am not placing the blame on the messengers as much as the message I falsely received.

The problem is that some of the messengers, who in many cases are bound to this spirit, are either unaware or unequipped to extricate those of us who are also bound to this monster called Mammon.

The motives of my heart were wrong and devious by listening to messages knowingly or not were steeped in the systems of Mammon. There are prosperity messages today that are so corrupted that it has polluted the purity of the truth.

The Bible principles are correct: Give and you shall receive; but most of our goals are not for the things above.

> If ye then be risen with Christ, seek those things that
> are above, where Christ sitteth on the right hand of

God. Set your affection on the things above, not on things on earth.

—*Colossians 3:1-2*

The reality is, we who are led by the Spirit are wealthy IN CHRIST. We are wealthy because everything He has, we have, if we truly belong to Him.

Dear reader whether you have a million dollars or barely enough food to eat, we are all in one way or another bound to Mammon. We are being led by a spirit, but what spirit, Is the question we must answer. And the Holy Spirit in His mercy is allowing us to see the truth.

How The Holy Spirit Changed My Master

The Holy Spirit began to "deal" with me after I repented. He came to me in gentle yet profound ways about my bondages and wrong thinking. He would show me the depths of my attachments to Mammon. Part of this teaching is a result of those sessions with my TRUE MASTER.

Mammon is only mentioned a few times in the scriptures. Yet it is the most insidious devil on this planet.

One way Jesus showed the world He would not be controlled by Mammon was to make Judas the ministry treasurer. How many ministers do you know who would look for a thief among their faithful followers and appoint him the guardian of the money? Jesus made a powerful statement, by doing this. Jesus understood His mission on the earth and showed His disciples how to establish His Father's Kingdom without bowing to Mammon.

We just read we can not serve two masters, because we will hate the one and love the other. This is because masters require undivided attention from their disciples. Jesus said "a house divided cannot stand."

The truth is, many of the so-called Christians, in reality do not love Jesus. They like Jesus but they love money. It is a sad thing to learn that those who profess to love Jesus in essence hate Him.

If we are bowing our knee to Mammon we hate Jesus. The Scripture makes it clear that we love one and hate the other. As you continue to read, you will see the seriousness of our betrayal. Judas only got thirty pieces of silver. What are we selling out for?

Why would Jesus ask Peter three times in John 21:15-17 if he loved Him? Jesus was using the Greek word for love, Agape, which means unselfish love. Peter was responding with the Greek word Phileo, which means affection without demonstration. The reason, as we have discussed before, is that love requires action. But liking someone does not demand a response from us.

Is it any wonder Jesus began His discourse in Matthew 6 with giving as the first and foremost sign of expressing what one verbalizes?

I learned it was not giving that was my problem, but the motive behind the gift. That was and is what is wrong with messages on prosperity today.

Giving is truly the beginning of all beginnings when it comes to demonstrating who we serve. But why we give will separate the wheat from the chaff, or God from Mammon.

We find in 1 Timothy 6:10 that the love of money is the root of all evil. This tells me that if someone is having problems in his life he should investigate the roots of the "flowering problems."

According to this Scripture we will discover that the love of money is the cause. This is Mammon controlling our lives and our attention.

Where your treasure is, there will be your heart also.

Let's be honest with ourselves and uncover why we do what we do.

Money decides how we dress so we can get that certain job. If we befriend certain people because of their influence and connections, then money is deciding who our friends are.

If we work extra long hours to maintain a lifestyle, then money is deciding how much time we will spend with our family.

If our wife works so we can be wealthier, then money has decided that our children are better off with someone other than their mother.

If we attend Churches whose main messages are prosperity and words that focus on me getting my needs met, then money and self are my motives, not what God might be saying to the nations.

The list goes on and on. Sermons that alter the very heart of the true gospel are negotiated with, in order that we might gain.

We are living in the age that can be described as Modern Apostate Christendom, which simply means willfully and purposely rejecting the teachings of Jesus.

Jesus said to seek first His kingdom and His righteousness and all these things shall be added but Mammon and the "Apostate Christendom" say, "Seek first financial security, and then you will have both time and money to give to the kingdom of God."

Apostate Christendom dressed up in the modern day prosperity message, has rewritten the scriptures into respectable "practical wisdom" about our finances. There seems to be a subliminal message, that gain is associated with super faith.

The statements Jesus makes in Matthew 6:25-33 are clear and uncompromising.

> Therefore I tell you, do not worry about your life, what you will eat or what you will drink, or about your body, what you will wear. Is not life more than food, and the body more than clothing? Look at the birds of the air; they neither sow nor reap nor gather into barns, and yet your heavenly Father feeds them. Are you not of more value than they? And can any of you by worrying add a single hour to your span of

life? And why do you worry about clothing? Consider the lilies of the field, how they grow; they neither toil nor spin, yet I tell you, even Solomon in all his glory was not clothed like one of these. But if God so clothes the grass of the field, which is alive today and tomorrow is thrown into the oven, will he not much more clothe you—you of little faith? Therefore do not worry, saying, "What will we eat?" or "What will we drink" or "What will we wear?" For it is the Gentiles who strive for all these things; and indeed your heavenly Father knows that you need all these things. But strive first for the kingdom of God and his righteousness, and all these things will be given to you as well.

Most of those words have become meaningless in Churches whose goals are primarily focused on prosperity. If anyone were dare to speak or act in the ways described above (take no thought for tomorrow), he would be labeled irresponsible, regarded unreliable and dismissed as a fool.

Verse 26 plainly states that our living is not dependent upon our working, and our future is not dependent upon our savings, but is solely dependent upon who our Father is.

Nevertheless, many modern day prophets and apostles speak about prosperity and wealth transfers as if they were the captain on the Titanic, imploring their passengers to put out the deck chairs and enjoy the voyage.

We were not confused about the meaning of these statements when we first read "lay not up for yourselves treasures upon the earth", or "take no thought for tomorrow," or "labor not for the meat which perishes" or "seek first the kingdom of God…." The confusion arises when our needs and wants become more important than our mental assent to God's word.

To hope, think and confess something according to our "faith"; but then choose to live according to Mammon's principles because of what we call "reality," is to live in hypocrisy. Can we honestly call that being a Christian?

The age in which we are living demands the Church to either serve God or take its chances with Mammon. The lifestyles of most professing Christians are barely distinguishable from "respectable heathenism".

Forgive me for speaking so bluntly, but we are living in dangerous times, and we need to change why we do what we do or we will hear the Lord say "DEPART FROM ME I NEVER KNEW YOU."

Many of us believe that the attack on the twin towers in New York, September 11, 2001 was God, telling us that Mammon was being judged, and all who continued to nurse from the paps of that god would suffer the same judgments. Study the eighteenth chapter of Revelation and see for yourself.

If we look at our life, we will see whom we are serving. We will hate the one (God) and love security (Mammon); or we will hold to God and despise Mammon or security in this world's system.

But why should we hate security in money? The Bible says "money answereth all things and money is a defense" (Ecclesiastes 10:19 and 7:12).

The use of money in these scriptures doesn't imply that those who use it have put their trust in it; rather that money serves them.

If we will take another look at Ecclesiastes 12:13, we will see that the conclusion of the matter is "Fear God, keep His commandments."

Proverbs 8:13 says, The fear of the Lord is to HATE EVIL. Evil can be defined as anything that demands our trust rather than God.

Proverbs 3:5-6 says, Trust in the Lord with all thine heart and lean not to thine own understanding.

ALL OF OUR HEART means all of our heart, which is what we have been attempting to liberate.

Commerce Of This World

This is the condition of the Church today relative to Mammon. Unfortunately we do not hate the systems of this world the way Jesus did. One of the best examples is given us in Matthew 21:12-13.

Then Jesus entered the temple and drove out all who were selling and buying in the temple, and he overturned the tables of the money changers and the seats of those who sold doves. He said to them, It is written,

> My house shall be called a house of prayer; But you are making it a den of robbers.

In 1 Cor. 3:16 we read how once we become the house for the Holy Spirit, we are then considered the temple of God.

Look closely at what Jesus is doing, **He is making a statement to all of those who use their temples for negotiating with Mammon for their security. The Holy Spirit of God will not share His domain with any other masters or idols.**

Jesus made a point of driving out those who were selling and buying. They were merchandising what is holy. It is an inner desire of a wicked heart to take from others, to gain at the expense of someone else, to lust for riches to satisfy the soul. It is the very love of money that is the root for all evil. It is part of the very seed of evil that corrupted Lucifer.

> Through the abundance of your commerce you were filled with lawlessness and violence and you sinned.
> —*Ezekiel 28:16 (Amplified Bible)*

This is the beginning of our exchange of masters. Selling and buying is the method of commerce in the system of Mammon. The Kingdom of God operates by Sowing and Reaping.

Jesus makes the statement in Luke 17:28-29, when asked when would the kingdom of God come: Likewise also as it was in the days of Lot: they did eat, they drank, they bought, they sold, they planted, they built: But the same day that Lot went out of Sodom it rained fire and brimstone from heaven, and destroyed them all. I believe the importance of the terms buying and selling indicate an individuals overall decision to trust in his own methods of conducting his life rather than trusting God. The illustration is so vivid in Mark 4:14-20 in which the condition of our hearts are such that the word of God can not find a place to be sown that it might reap the 30, 60, and 100 fold return. This demonstrates to me that our minds and hearts are so preoccupied with providing our own resources through the systems of this world namely buying and selling, selling and buying that to trust our lives to the principles of sowing and reaping are very difficult in deed.

I am not saying that all of us who buy and sell are serving Mammon. I am simply stating that this type of living demonstrates where our trust lie.

After Jesus makes the statement of the two masters he went on to say,

> And the Pharisees also, who were covetous, heard all these things: and they derided him. And he said unto them, Ye are they which justify yourselves before men; but God knoweth your hearts: for that which is highly esteemed among men is abomination in the sight of God.
>
> —*Luke 16:14-15*

Let's examine more closely the word "covetousness." Look in Joshua at the seriousness of God towards this sin.

The following are the instructions given to Israel on taking the wealth from Jericho after the battle:

And ye, in any wise keep yourselves from the accursed thing, lest ye make yourselves accursed, when ye take of the accursed thing, and make the camp of Israel a curse, and trouble it. But all the silver, and gold, and vessels of brass and iron, are consecrated unto the LORD: they shall come into the treasury of the LORD.

—*Joshua 6:18-19*

We know the story of how Achan (means serpent), who took the accursed things from Jericho and caused the death of 36 men of Israel at Ai.

Look at what Achan said to Joshua, "When I saw among the spoils a goodly Babylonian garment, and two hundred shekels of silver, a wedge of Gold worth fifty shekels, I COVETED THEM."

This story contains so many truths that it would require another book to explore them all. Let me point out some things relevant to our study.

God hates the system of Babylon. It is the system of Mammon perpetrated by buying and selling and it is built upon covetousness and greed.

As much as God loves Man, He hates evil more, which He demonstrates by the deaths of the innocent soldiers as the consequence of the sin of Achan.

When Jesus told the Pharisees who were covetous that what they found valuable was an abomination to God, it was not because of the gold, silver and bronze but because of their hearts. It is not the gold and silver that was wrong. It is to what master they are consecrated.

Jesus drove the robbers and thieves from the temple because of their hearts and the god they served. Remember, we are His temple, and He is a jealous God.

In my life I refuse to buy what I don't need, and I will not sell what I don't want. I prefer to give away what still has value. I believe many Christians live this way but there are some who are preoccupied with buying and selling.

The book of Revelation 13:17 makes a very strong statements: So that no one can buy or sell who does not have the mark, that is, the name of the beast or the number of its name.

As I said earlier the terms buying and selling do not make you the servant of Mammon but our hearts demonstrate which is our master, the beast or Jesus The Christ.

This means to me, that if we, as the true body of Christ do not learn how to operate in the supernatural, we will be martyred or bow to the idol, which I believe is Mammon..

I am convinced that sowing and reaping is the way of supplying the needs of the kingdom of God. Unfortunately, many of the ministries who are adept at using these terms do not operate under these principles.

In most cases, their methods of sowing and reaping are mingled with the "commerce system of the world."

The machinery of the ministry has become so conformed to the systems of the world that in order to do business they begin to rely on wrong models. Confidence subtly shifts from faith in God to faith in proven business principles. The results are temporarily sound and effective for the purpose of saving money. This allows the Ministries to preach the gospel to the lost, which appears good. But what we are finding is real problems. "The lost" the major ministries are converting, sadly fail to come out from the system of Mammon. The real tragedy is that they really do not even know the difference between the two Kingdoms.

The new converts are trained more by what they see than what they hear. The ministers are preaching true principles from the word of God. But the converts see most of the ministries on TV always asking for money. They see the methods the Christian Church is using to "raise funds." and see little if any difference with other worldly fund raising events, other than the promise of getting a return on your gift.

The so called Christians they produce are hybrid forms of the world system. They become trained in Church language and appearances without changing the allegiances to the god they have been serving, Mammon. This is not a condemnation but the sad truth for many of the Churches in the Western world.

The need for money is real. The hearts of the ministers are pure for the most part. But because we have all drunk from the cup of abominations spoken of in Revelation 17:2, we are intoxicated with ideas and methods from this world.

We are all to blame for the condition of the Church. We all feel helpless to change the overpowering demand of more and more money to feed "the machine."

So the question we must all answer is how can we live in this world and not conform to its systems and methods of doing business?

Come Ye Out My People

And he cried mightily with a loud voice, saying, Babylon the great is fallen, is fallen, and has become a dwelling place of demons, a prison for every foul spirit, and a cage for every unclean and hated bird! For all the nations have drunk of the wine of the wrath of her fornication, the kings of the earth have committed fornication with her, and the merchants of the earth have become rich through the abundance of her luxury. And I heard another voice from heaven saying, Come out of her, my people, lest you share in her sins, and lest you receive of her plagues.

—*Revelation 18:2-4*

The only person that overcame this world was Jesus. The methods He used must be what we use. He said in Luke 16 that if we are faithful with unrighteous Mammon we will graduate to receive "true riches." The true riches are not material, such as gold and silver, but rather our trust in the Holy Spirit contained within our hearts.

And if you are untrustworthy about worldly wealth,
who will trust you with the true riches of heaven?

—*Luke 16:11*

As hard as this is to say, the only reason we as the Church
are not operating with the true riches is because we have
not been faithful with the unrighteous Mammon.

We have coveted it and indeed sought ways of having
both this world's riches, here and in the world to come.
Babylon is being judged again and all who operate in its
system of commerce and trust will suffer the same consequences.

The more I understand the Scriptures, the more truth
is revealed to me about the term "true riches." I believe it
is the same thing Paul was speaking about in Ephesians in
chapters 1 and 3 when he spoke of the riches of His glory.

We have seen over and over again the value placed on
the heart of man by God. The scripture that says where
your heart is will be the place of your treasure. The heart
of man is the place where God or Mammon deposit the
currency of our trust. We then have access to the kingdom
of God and the true riches or the kingdom of this world
and sure destruction.

The "true riches" are the hearts of God's children who
are totally His. In those hearts God will deposit all the
riches of Himself. What can Mammon offer that is more
valuable than that?

"Lord, I repent, help us all to see the truth of your word and have the faith to operate in this world and not be conformed to it; this is my prayer.

Yesterday's Temptations The Same As Today

If we can learn nothing else during this discussion let us observe our Lord's response to this world's wealth and the call of Mammon.

Observe carefully the lessons Jesus was teaching us through His wilderness temptation with Satan:

Then the Spirit led Jesus into the desert to be tempted by the devil. Jesus ate nothing for forty days and nights. After this, he was very hungry. The devil came to Jesus to tempt him, saying," If you are the Son of God, tell these rocks to become bread."

Jesus answered, "It is written in the Scriptures, A person does not live by eating only bread, but by everything God says.'

Then the devil led Jesus to the holy city of Jerusalem and put him on a high place of the Temple. The devil said, "If you are the Son of God, jump down, because it is written in the Scriptures:

He has put his angels in charge of you.
They will catch you in their hands
so that you will not hit your foot on a rock.
(Psalm 91:11–12)

Jesus answered him, "It also says in the Scriptures, 'Do not test the Lord your God.'"

Then the devil led Jesus to the top of a very high mountain and showed him all the kingdoms of the world and all their splendor. The devil said, "If you will bow down and worship me, I will give you all these things."

Jesus said to the devil, "Go away from me, Satan! It is written in the Scriptures, 'You must worship the Lord your God and serve only him.'"

—*Matthew 4:1-10*

We should really study that sequence of events in the Scriptures. Satan begins with temptation of the flesh, (food). The body and flesh of man is the first and easiest place for attacks from the enemy.

Our weakness as men has always originated through the sense gates, (seeing, hearing, feeling, smelling and tasting). Where was the first and most costly temptation for man? In the Garden Eden, Eve was enticed through her eyes and stomach before Satan could seduce her mind.

Study Genesis 3 to see how she was convinced through her senses before being persuaded by her mind.

The next attempt was with religion, which is for the soul, comprised of our mind, heart and emotions.

You notice how Satan quoted scriptures to show us how spiritual he is? This is a lesson for all of us. Just because we can conform a scripture to our belief system does not mean that God is approving, our lie as His truth.

There are many "New Age" followers, and cults, who can quote Scripture to support their hierarchy. The Bible is written for man to discover the truth in the person of Jesus. Not so man can justify his behavior or introduce another religion to satisfy the longing of the soul.

The Temple is a design of God and is the invisible symbol of the Temple which houses the Holy Spirit within each of us who belong to Him. There are history books filled with stories of how people died for their belief in a religion. Monks and Buddhist priests even have set themselves on fire. Today Muslims turn themselves into suicide bombers believing they are pleasing Allah. Satan is still using the same methods to tempt God (Matthew 4:7).

The final test for every man is whom will we worship? The worship from man has been the desire of Satan from the day iniquity was found in him (Ezekiel. 28:15). He still promises to every man who will worship him "riches and kingdoms." This is not different in our days, only the disguise is in prosperity and the spirit Satan uses is Mammon.

This sequence has not changed over the centuries. Our bodies and our souls are still the place most vulnerable to the assault of Satan.

So, instead of our using the Holy Spirit and the word of God to equip and train ourselves for the Kingdom of God, we turn to this world's system and the anti-Christ himself taking the form of Mammon.

Mammon's goal is first to seduce us through promises of gain, which appeals to our fleshly appetites.

Then when we belong to him demonstrated through our trusts, he terrifies us through the fears of loss. This method is easily achieved by painting pictures in our minds and hearts of doing without anything we believe we must have to survive.

This picture of losing is a conditioned behavior within all of us-to elicit fear and anxiety.

Notice the sequence of his assault on theSon of God and recall the way Jesus outlined his teachings in Matthew 6.

Battle Between What Master To Trust

The battle is ultimately between "trust" in this world and "faith" in God. Trust in what we can see, feel and control versus faith in what God says is our heritage by covenant.

The economics of this world are perpetrated through health care, education, politics and religion. The system relies on the trust of the people to perpetuate the lie. The lie is other things than God can be our security. The truth is few really believe that God can take care of us in all circumstances, so they work for money because they believe that with enough, we will be "safe."

You and I will continually be challenged to live by faith in God or by trust in this world's system, known as Mammon. These challenges may be obstacles that appear to be locked doors. The keys we use to unlock those doors are manufactured by fear or created by our faith.

If we use the keys produced by our faith, we will walk through doors that open into limitless possibilities with God, and our faith will grow strong like muscles through exercise.

We will learn the difference between slaves and stewards. We will move into the arena of decisions that constitute real change in our cities. I am not necessarily referring to politics.

If we see our life has no longer our own, belonging to the only true King of Kings, our vessels become His. Then we can fulfill our destiny by becoming first servants and then true disciples of God.

Then our faith will become transformed to something that has substance. This substance is the very essence of God.

We are then the Master's Key. He has been seeking a generation He could trust with the Keys of His Kingdom. "The Key of David" is the closest thing we can compare to this level of authority.

You and I have not yet known the possibilities that are our inheritance when we no longer belong to the god of this world.

However, if we use the keys of fear, we will open the doors to smaller and smaller prison cells until at last we are like animals in a zoo. Each cell will be smaller than the last because we can not serve two masters and the master we have chosen wants prisoners, not servants.

We should not be deceived; Mammon has keys for the doors of its kingdom. Its kingdom is constructed in shadows, lies and slieght of hand. It is built upon the blood of men and women who have devoted their lives to building their foundations of "security" on shifting sands and greedy desires.

The keys in Mammon's kingdom are simple. Believe in only what you can "see, feel, hear, taste and control." Trust in nothing that pressures you to give or infringes upon your security. The foundations of this belief are fear, selfishness, covetousness, lying and hate. Its fruit is restlessness, illness, suffering loss and death.

The kingdom of this world is determined to fascinate everyone with its riches and beauty. The hypnotic allure of this kingdom is the illusion of wealth, riches and power.

Then many swallow the bait and run after false promises of power and wealth. The amazing thing about the people who become hooked is that they willingly risk all they own for the chance of becoming independently wealthy. Is it any wonder that gambling and lotteries are sweeping the world?

The real irony and tragedy is that statistics show that 90+% of those who win these lotteries become alcoholics, drug addicts, divorced, or commit suicide.

A New Generation

This is the generation that will witness the "Daniels" living in Babylon "who know their God will be strengthened and do great exploits." But when we read the rest of that story, we find that there is a cost to those who are wise.

Many will lose their lives trying to bring out those in captivity. This is not a popular prosperity message. But, praise God, Daniel 12:3 says:

> Everyone who has been wise will shine as bright as the sky above, and everyone who has led others to please God will shine like the stars.

As I have said, the issue is not now, nor has it ever been, about money. It is about whom you have trusted and obeyed.

Come out of the land of your broken cisterns and unfulfilled destinies. What visions are you running after? Are you living as a spectator of those who are running the race set before them? Are you not tired of merely watching the show, and paying for it? Should you not be warring against the religious spirits who have made you passive and stolen your resolve?

Awake! Oh men and women of God and war against the subtlest of enemies within our souls, Mammon and the system it represents.

The time is short. The hour is much later than you have believed or prepared for. Hear the watchman's call before it is too late. You have been bought with a price more costly than all the gold and silver you could hope to possess.

There is an end-time deliverance of wealth that will truly be transferred to the righteous. The qualification is a radical change in your life styles and affections. Do not underestimate the power of the Holy Spirit to help you. You have believed the lies of the enemy and have surrendered without firing a shot. I tell you now under the authority of the most high God, Thus says the Lord: "You have been born for a time such as this. If you refuse to fight for your rightful inheritance, I will find another generation that will take the challenge and posses the land."

Abraham, Isaac and Jacob faced the same devils you are faced with, and became heroes of the faith. God is saying, "I have given you more weapons, more truth and more promises."

We have no excuses. God will have someone He can trust and I purpose to be one whom He can count.

For I truly recognize the truth that drives me: "those who have been forgiven much love much". And now I can and will say to Jesus: "I can never repay you for what you did but I willing give you what you purchased?"

What about you?

Conclusion

This has been a book that has not been easy to write. I believe that with the guidance of the Holy Spirit and prayers of the saints something positive will have been the result.

I have understood so well that our Lord designed Matthew chapter 6 with you and me in His mind. I observed how He brought me from my weak understanding of giving to the powerful levels of becoming the gift. I did not even understand what that meant until I began to study the Scriptures. I could see clearly that everything I have belongs to Him and the only way I can approach His altar is with me as the gift.

It sounded egotistical at first, until I began to understand the love contained within His cross. His love for me took Him through Gethsemane to the cross. Someone as unworthy as me could capture the Father's heart to send His Son to such a death.

The places the Holy Spirit took me were so extraordinary that this life no longer held any fascination. In fact, if the Body of Christ could ever truly see the power in yielding up our life to gain His, chains that bind them would fall off and the grip of Mammon would be destroyed once and for all.

How could I withhold anything from a love such as this?

The more I studied chapter 6 of Matthew, the more I could see the design of prayer. Real prayer is not possible without first understanding giving. The truth is that the Church, who longs to walk in the power of prayer, has been hindered because of their unwillingness to give.

Prayer, the backbone of our life with God, has been void of any real power. This is because we are a Church that is selfish and stingy with something that does not even belong to us.

Then the Lord revealed the prayer of Stephen to me. How this prayer released a religious man name Saul into a spiritual giant named Paul. How the destiny of Stephen was fulfilled through the life of Paul. The depths of a man's prayers are not limited to the temporal time he lives on the earth. For example when Moses asked God to show him His glory, God allowed Moses to see the transfiguration of Jesus thousands of years after he asked.

These are the prayers that move God and shake earth. These are the prayers the Church must enter, if we are to see the great awakening before the return of our Lord.

Then the Lord allowed me to understand fasting from both a biblical point and personal perspective in my own life. Over the years I have observed my times spent with the Lord while fasting to be the most revelatory. This I believe is for many reasons, but primarily it is because the major weapon of the enemy is neutralized during these times. Life in the flesh has lost its appeal, thus removing the artillery from the hands of the devil.

I realize I have just scratched the surface of this major weapon and am eagerly awaiting the next stages of development in this area of my growth.

I see how Matthew 6 is strategically designed to prepare us for the battle of all battles, with Mammon. This spirit has feasted on the saints over the centuries and has increased the pressure 100 fold in the past few years.

This battle requires all of the keys we have received from giving, praying and fasting. Those keys were designed to show us where we have been held captive. These keys are designed specifically for every believer to uncover within their souls the depths of our deceptions.

These keys will show us how our thought life has contaminated our hearts and taken us from innocence to hardened hearts. These keys can open the doors but we must have the courage to change what we find inside. If we are willing to allow the Spirit of God to do surgery upon our hearts we can win the battle against Mammon.

Finally, we must become The Master's Key. This key is only given to those who have proven that their life does not belong to them. This key will close those doors within us from ever bowing to Mammon again. This key will open the door to the Holy Spirit to use us to set many captives free.

It is my prayer that you will use this book as a means of discovering your real potential as a child of the King. You will use this book to recognize every instance in which you have bowed to Mammon, and repent. I hope we can all see how far we have strayed from the truth of the Gospel and return before it is too late.

My prayer for all of us is that God in His mercy will grant us time and energy to change; Love and grace to be a light in the darkness; Power and might to hate evil, and truth and righteousness to live a Holy life before His return.

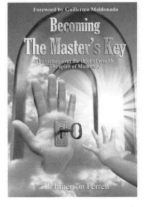